THE ART

TRANSFORMATIONAL

CHANGE

A HANDBOOK FOR MANAGERS AND LEADERS

KETAN VARIA

The Art of Transformational Change
A Handbook For Managers and Leaders
Copyright © 2015 by Ketan Varia All rights reserved.
First Print Edition: September 2015

Published by Kinetik Solutions
Cover and Formatting by Streetlight Graphics
www.streetlightgraphics.com
Illustrations by Joe Evans www.quirkyjoe.com

ISBN: 978-0-9932390-0-7

To my grandmother Santaben Mansang Varia,
whose blessings have made my life unfold in a
positive way. Having lived in three continents, she
has developed traits that have given her life a solid
foundation. Santaben has always adapted herself to
any given situation, demonstrated intense willpower
based on faith and developed a high awareness
of the power of relationships. Above all, she has
always been tolerant to all, by understanding
their points of view and accepting difference.

And to all people who are always open
to new ideas and ways of thinking.

CONTENTS

ACKNOWLEDGEMENTS

It was Isaac Newton who said, "If I have seen further than others, it is by standing on the shoulders of giants". I give credit to all of those 'giants' for my being able to write this book. Firstly Dr W. Edwards Deming, whose work on understanding variation and 14 principles of management made a seminal difference in my early career. Dr Russ Ackoff, who I was lucky enough to meet, and whose work on systems thinking and decision making helped me develop my consultancy work. Dr Edward de Bono's books which have helped me understand new ways of thinking around any situation. The Soviet Inventor Altshuller for his inventive thinking in new products, which is something that has been under-utilised in today's world, and to Taichi Ohno, considered to be the father of the Toyota Production System, which became known as 'Lean'. A special thanks to Dr Bill Bellows who has provided some 'light bulb moments', always ready to listen to my ideas, but challenging them in a way that brought new insight for me.

There are several people who have given direct support to this book. Lynn Ashburner, David Shaked and Paul Frobisher for their insight and feedback on early chapters. Ade McCormack, Alan Finn and David

Thomson for their encouragement. Joe Evans for supplying the graphics that go with the words. Alisha Nurse for helping me with getting this book published. Also thanks to various people who have provided research and editorial support over a period of time including Shelagh Aitken, Caroline Appleby, Mounia Bencheqroun, Sanjiv Bhardwaj, Bhavisa Bhardwaj, Robyn Brown, Nadia David, Anooj Dodhia, Fiona Dowling, Matthew Gibson, Jayni Gudka, Layla Hendow, Pooja Jain, Charlotte Jennings, Denis Judge, Suzanne Kilele, Jodie McIlwain, Mahersh Shah, Nishma Shah, Jiani Qian, Rishabh Varia, Kruti Varia and David Williams.

FOREWORD

To the casual observer, every organisation, from for-profit to non-profit, from public to private, from manufacturing to city government, is unique. Each with its own vision, strategy, and operating policies, both formal and informal. Each with its own customers and suppliers, as well as management hierarchy. Yet, upon closer examination, there are patterns at work, guided by the "theories-in-use" of everyone in an organisation, that allow for categories to appear and similarities to emerge. Gradually, organisations that may well have started small, perhaps in a garage, with enormous fanfare and success, become siloed and slow, if not resistant to change. In a simple model, I place them in the category of "Organisations as Usual". Instead of managing interdependence, they manage the parts "taken separately", to borrow from Dr Russell Ackoff. Instead of thriving, they struggle to survive, ever in reaction to emerging problems, as well as a changing marketplace. Along the way, problems persist; fragmentation increases, teamwork decreases, and old customers depart. If fortunate, new customers replace the departed, yet the cycle continues.

In my experience in studying organisations for the past 25 years, "Usual" organisations favour results over process. That is, there is generally little interest in "by what method?" to quote W. Edwards Deming. Yet, without a method, how would "Organisations as Usual" transform to "Organisations as Unusual"? Chapter by chapter in this book Ketan Varia presents a well-established collection of techniques and strategies to counteract these forces of decay, enabling "Organisations as Usual" to change course and continuously transform into "Organisations as Unusual".

Readers will enjoy Ketan's steady use of everyday examples to illustrate a foundational set of strategies and techniques, covering topics ranging from innovation to systems thinking and fast learning. Readers will also quickly sense the comfort with which Ketan has led the implementation of these concepts with his clients, concepts he has lived and mastered. With this book, he has crafted a leader's guide to successful transformational change, designed for beginners and veterans alike. Let the journey begin!

Dr Bill Bellows
Los Angeles, California. USA.
5 May 2015.

INTRODUCTION

Almost fifty-nine percent of corporations fail to meet at least one of their transformational change objectives.[1] While more than one in five organisations go through some kind of transformational programme to improve performance, a study by McKinsey found that only thirty percent of change programmes were deemed successful[2]; and a study by Moorhouse Consulting found that fifty-three percent of FTSE 250 organisations delivered change programmes late.[3]

Organisations large and small, public and private, autocratic and democratic, have been consistently unable to apply lessons from the past and achieve success in change programmes. Large corporations may fail to deliver satisfactory benefits even when huge resources are expended and the benefits obvious. In many cases this is because the case studies and methodologies used by guides on change are not universally appropriate or transferable. Methodologies

1 Hans Jorgenson, Lawrence Owen and Andreas Neus, Making Change Work: Global Study, (New York: IBM Global Services, 2008).

2 Scott Keller and Carolyn Aiken, The Inconvenient Truth about Change, (McKinsey & Company, 2008).

3 Moorhouse Consulting, "Change-ready and agile organisations are more likely to experience growth", Barometer of Change, (Moorhouse Consulting May 2013).

are not wrong or misguided; they just can't be applied to all organisations.

Organisational cultures differ; change programmes must relate to each individual circumstance. Managers may not know which methods work in their organisation. In many cases, change leaders are unaware of failure until a major evaluation takes place, which can make the situation even worse.

The Art of Transformational Change: A Handbook for Managers and Leaders, is a handbook for managers and leaders involved in, or contemplating, a change or transformation programme. It provides a practical, detailed and informed framework for creating a change process. This handbook distils tried-and-tested techniques from the multitude of solutions available. Through step-by-step instructions and visual illustrations, it guides the user through context-specific techniques that can be uniquely tailored to any organisational change programme.

What is transformational change?

All large organisations are likely to be going through some change including IT systems, new products, new structures, or in some cases, a new vision. Transformational change is when the change impacts more than the day-to-day process of the work, but requires new types of thinking and behaviours as the change itself cannot survive or be sustained without the latter.

What is leadership?

I have written this book for managers and non-managers alike. Anyone who can influence change and lead it, actively engages with others and seeks participation with collaboration is in my mind a leader. Leadership is about working with people as they are, with their expertise, relationships and insight, and a deep sense of wanting to change "together". This is supported by leadership experts like Scholtes.[4] It isn't about the thumping boss, about a winner take all, or about "forcing" change. Leadership skills most in need are ones around coaching and being resourceful. Leaders understand the processes in place in an organisation and the dynamics between them, including interdependencies, i.e. they have a more holistic picture of what happens in an organisation. This is often referred to as systems thinking.

The interventions in each chapter of this book are to be used by a leader together with the people he or she influences to provide that deeper insight during a change programme.

Chapter 1 examines the dimensions of value to ensure customer perceptions are effectively captured. Chapter 2 examines the importance of clear-outs of both materials and information in organisations. Chapter 3 looks at RACI, a tool which helps codify "who does what" in any change programme while in Chapter 4, we look at setting up continuous review in organisations. Chapter 5 looks at the creation and dismantling of high performance teams. In Chapter 6, TRIZ, an innovative

---

4 Scholtes, Peter R. The Leader's Handbook: Making things happen, getting things done. New York: McGraw-Hill, 1998.

way of problem-solving is discussed that offers low cost solutions to issues arising in change programmes. Chapter 7 discusses systems thinking, which allows the understanding of joins in complex transformation: what impacts what, even if the level of impact is ambiguous and finally, Chapter 8 looks at fast failure and fast learning in process design within transformation.

The weaknesses of existing ways of working become obvious when an organisation is seeking large-scale or transformational change. Creative thinking and ingenuity are needed to attain organisational benefits in areas where there are few margins for error; the survival of the whole organisation, rather than a single part, may be at stake. Leaders need to be aware of both the reasons for, and context of, the change in its preparation stage, and also appropriate highly leveraged methods and tools that give the change process direction and ultimately, success. They also need to be aware that, even when the change programme results in short-term success, it is not the end of the story: sustainability must be an integral part of the change.

Change approaches, such as project or resource planning, risk and issue management or performance indicators, are often disconnected. *The Art of Transformational Change: A Handbook for Managers and Leaders* is a powerful book focusing on a proven, holistic approach to implementing, dealing with and adapting to change. All transformation programmes need three elements to succeed: planning for transformation; processes and methods to achieve change; and a plan for sustainability. This book provides techniques that are useful across all three areas.

Evaluations can provide powerful analysis after the event, but few are actively used during a transformation programme. The aim of this book is to give change leaders tools and concepts to use during the process, in the "heat of the moment", to provide assurance and creative thought about the organisation's transformation.

Of the many techniques available to change leaders, I have chosen the eight that in my experience have been the most effective in providing a "better picture" and shedding light on change programmes. The techniques themselves are not complex, and have been distilled from decades of hands-on experience. They have been proven, through use by many organisations, to be both effective and beneficial.

Transformational excellence in an organisation is the result of outstanding teamwork and skilful adjustments to the programme, rather than top-down command-and-control or bottom-up training and motivation investment approaches.

The Art of Transformational Change: A Handbook for Managers and Leaders offers managers the opportunity to learn important lessons which will help them avoid mistakes, and even more, apply right practice to planning for change in their organisations.

CHAPTER 1
Using Dimensional Values

Value has many dimensions. This chapter explores effective ways of using an organisation's resources to deliver value in terms of client satisfaction gained from efficient service delivery. The content has been based on the work of Professor Noriaki Kano.

Thought or consideration is rarely given to all the dimensions of value to the end customer of large-change projects. These consumers experience several aspects, intentional and unintentional, of a product or service change as a result of the transformation.

Transformation goals are often internally driven (e.g. cutting cost, accelerating product delivery, better dissemination of information), but rarely are these translated into "value" as perceived by the customer. Transformational change can provide the opportunity to look for and understand not just the organisation internally, but their clients' and customers' insights for value, and to ask whether the impetus for change meets everyone's needs.

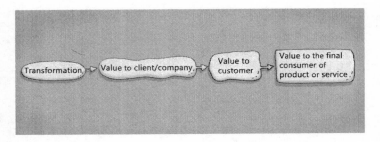

Figure 1: How transformation benefits the final consumer

All organisations have a chain of customers. Understanding this chain and customer benefit as perceived by value at each stage needs to be considered and appreciated. Those driving transformational change need to ensure value throughout the chain of change that results in benefiting the final consumer. One example might be a train operator who finds out that their business customers expect to have access to Wi-Fi and 3G to remain in touch. Virgin Trains recognised this and now ensure that a 3G signal exists on many of its services.

Figure 2: Understanding true needs of the customer

When the different perspectives of "value" for the products or service between the company, customer, and stakeholders are resolved and the expectation clearly managed, there is a ground-breaking benefit to the overall system. Value-engineering has provided models to design consumer products that include many dimensions to meet a variety of needs. In transformational change we build on this model so that the end value of the transformation is clearly articulated in a way that ensures true value is delivered and there is a focus on the areas that "really matter".

The four dimensions of value

All products or services have a variety of implicit or explicit functions. Each of these four functions fulfils a particular need: basic, satisfying, attractive and indifferent.

1. **Basic features:** These are the elements of the service that are taken for granted. There is huge dissatisfaction if these features are missing or if performance is poor. Often these elements are assumed, so "basic" features are not explicitly stated: when booking a plane flight, an airline's poor safety record would cause dissatisfaction. However, a good safety record would not necessarily result in a "satisfied" customer response. The customer's focus would likely be on other factors, perhaps check-in queues, on-board service and luggage handling. In the service industry, basic features may include timeliness as well as "softer" areas such as being polite and professional.

2. **Satisfying features:** Satisfaction and dissatisfaction with these features change in line with availability and performance: the more customers have of these features, the more satisfaction they get. It is often seen as the key feature in a sales pitch. In the airline industry this might be the amount of leg space for business travellers or the price for economy-class travellers. Another example of satisfying features could be "zero to sixty" acceleration performance of a car: the faster the acceleration, the more satisfied the customer will be. There is a clear linear link between satisfaction and the amount of this feature that exists: the more there is of this particular feature, the more satisfied the customer is.

3. **Attractive features:** The service user perceives these features as being unusually high in value; having them available will create an unexpected delight factor. These are often latent, unconscious desires which, once recognised, fulfil a hidden need. For example, an attractive feature for some customers would be a low-cost airline which offers a "kids board first" option, or a bank which delivers flowers on a customer's birthday.

Dimension	Outpatient X-ray service	Low-cost airline
Basic	Preparation prior to X-ray understood	Assigned seating
	Expected length of wait communicated	Safety to international standards
Satisfying	The shorter the wait, the better	Airport close to city
	Speed in receiving results	Variety of on-board paid snacks
	Inexpensive car park	On time arrival
Attractive/Delight	Walk-in service	Children board first
	Results given instantly	New planes
Indifferent	A letter with a fixed date of appointment	Hot meals on short-haul flights

Table 1: Examples of a value matrix for two different products

4. **Indifferent features:** These are not elements that the service user does not value; these elements of service were introduced at some time in the past because of customer requests, or were seen by the company as a way of differentiating themselves. With a true understanding of the customer's needs through research (whether via customer feedback or market research), it can become clear that little value is currently placed on these service features.

Let's consider the example of business travellers, who stay for a short stint (one or two nights) and are likely to be in the hotel (excluding sleeping time) for less than three hours in a day. They are also likely to be driven by efficiency and not attached to one particular hotel brand. What kind of satisfaction/dissatisfaction attributes might there be for these customers? Quick checkout, access to a desk and plenty of power sockets, a good mobile phone signal might become as important to them as room service. However they might be indifferent to features such as a bath, an external dial telephone line or even a good view. Satisfying features might include a range of TV channels, the ability to change temperature of the room and access to a restaurant. Attractive or delight features could be free WiFi, free converter sockets for international travellers or room service.

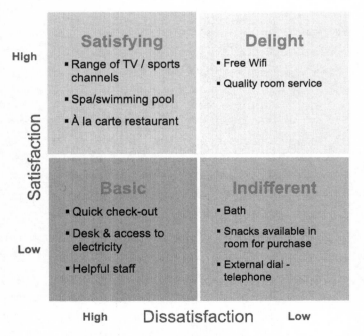

Figure 3: Satisfaction/dissatisfaction grid:
Hotel facilities for business travellers

Managing expectations

Some of the features customers expect may not be able to be met because of cost. Most London Underground passengers expect trains to run on time every day. However, the age of London Underground's infrastructure makes this unachievable. As a consequence, London Underground has trained its drivers to make an announcement every time their train is delayed, updating customers frequently to manage expectations. Most customers whose expectations are managed clearly and upfront, or are provided with an alternative, will accommodate service disruption. Similarly, in healthcare, informing people of the length of the time they need to wait at an outpatient clinic on arrival manages their expectations of the service. An ample supply of newspapers and magazines as well as health information and a coffee machine may also help.

The four dimensions of value can be dynamic and can vary for different customers. In some cases, a satisfying feature for one group of customers may be a basic feature for another group. This can occur when a public service, a hospital for example, is not tailored around customer demands, but around supply constraints. A basic feature for some patients may be having transport organised for them (e.g. for the elderly or non-drivers), while for others this may be a satisfying but not basic feature (e.g. busy working people) as they have a variety of alternatives.

Even a birthday cake could have different features to cater for the value by the customer, in this case a young child. Cakes can have different features with value determined by the child.

Figure 4: Features for a birthday cake

From attractive features to satisfying features

Over time features follow a maturity curve in which attractive features can become basic. Features become socialised: what was once deemed attractive becomes the norm, as can be seen clearly in the rapid development of new technology. A mobile phone alone is no longer enough, it needs additional features such as access to the internet, social media and email to satisfy customers. These may have been attractive features ten years ago; now they are merely satisfying.

From satisfying features to basic features

With time, many satisfying features become basic features: a mobile phone that can be carried in a pocket for example, or the ability to choose a particular hospital for elective surgery.

The recognition of the different types of value customers

get from different features can enable a company to modify their product range to create an entirely new product. For certain customers, satisfying features may be stripped from a product to create a new market for a more basic and cheaper product. Low-cost airlines are a good example: satisfying features such as on-board refreshments, extra legroom or allowances for checked-in baggage have been stripped away to create new demands in value for customers who require "no frills". This has resulted in the number of people flying to Europe from the UK growing by seventy percent between 1995 and 2010.[5] Equally, adding attractive features to an existing product can also create a new market: economy-plus seating now offers extra legroom and seat size on planes at a lower cost than first or business class.

Changing product features in a controlled way can help an organisation find a new market. Price reduction can be used to create a "segment" for a certain product by removing its attractive features and reducing its satisfying ones, while the basic ones remain the same. This is how low-cost airlines started. Sainsbury's the UK supermarket chain, has created an attractive feature whereby a customer asking for the location of a product is taken directly to the aisle and shelf, no matter how busy the staff are. This attractive feature is appealing in customer service and a clear differentiator for customers.

---

5 Rachael Harker and Tom Rutherford, 'Air transport statistics – Commons Library Standard Note', Parliament.uk, 13th June 2011 http://www.parliament.uk/briefing-papers/SN03760/air-transport-statistics [accessed 03/07/2014].

Value analysis: asking the right questions

Understanding the perceived values and dimensions of customer needs helps to better answer the following questions:

- What features should a product or service focus on, based on understanding what customers value?

- What use of resources will give the best returns in terms of perceived quality of service and satisfaction?

- Where do customer expectations need to be managed?

- Which elements of services can be downgraded?

- Which elements can be adapted, based on individuals or smaller groups of customers?

- Where should staff training and behaviour be focused?

The answers to these questions provide a better strategic fit between a product's features and fulfilment. They are defined through consultation with the customer. Any work that is not aligned with these results is unlikely to add value for the organisation or the customer.

How to discover the value features

Several steps are needed to identify explicit and implicit customer needs. An effective way of discovering these features is to record customer experience stories that describe the end-to-end process, so all relevant features will be articulated and captured. Another method is to look at customer complaints, which may well highlight latent needs that are not being met. The results of generic customer surveys can be used to uncover future needs for a service. In large-scale transformations, identifying these needs is essential not only for the immediate customer, but also for the end customer.

Once a list of features has been established, a satisfaction survey can be devised to enable features to be prioritised as: a) basic, b) satisfying, c) attractive or d) indifferent. Questionnaires need to ask both a positive and a negative question around each feature. Not just "how do you feel about having this feature?" but also "how do you feel about *not* having this feature?"

One quick way of finding the importance of each dimension is to arrange a workshop with customers. They could then be asked to identify basic, satisfying, attractive and indifferent elements. For the elements that are satisfying, deeper questions can reveal features to which they are indifferent. For example, an airline customer may have stated that they want hot food as a satisfying part of value, but if this service isn't there then how much would they miss it? When the full value elements have been clearly defined, dynamic workshops help place the service features into one of these dimensions.

Managing value conflicts

Various stakeholders may hold different value perceptions around the same service. A clear conflict between customer, organisation, employee or other stakeholder expectations must be managed. Take, for example, the service feature "delay-free trains".

Customer	Organisation	Employee
Basic requirement No delays on trains.	**Satisfying requirement** Keep track and signal defects to a minimum.	**Attractive requirement** If the trains run without delays, passengers should be pleased! **Basic requirement** Request not to take frustration for delays out on rail employees.

Table 2: Managing conflict by understanding expectations

Table 2 shows that expectation can be managed by continuously informing customers of the reason for delays, the possible length of delay and alternative travel options. Employees need to be trained to manage the situation. There also needs to be clear communication that incidents of aggression will not be tolerated.

Personalising value

Personalising value for individual customer groups, or even individuals, is the next stage. Different aspects of service elements can be extracted to meet the basic, satisfying and attractive value elements. Alternatively, customers can select a range from a list of all the value elements. Customers may well be willing to pay for additional features, the model used by low-cost airlines. The issue here is that customers distinguish between different value levels: they may be willing to pay for additional special features, but object strongly when those features are seen as basic.

Hotels that serve both business and leisure customers often have a variety of dining options, with different elements that are attractive to each group. This might include a choice of restaurant, bar snacks and room service. Holiday Inn, recognising that people might have different requirements for pillows, allows customers to order them on arrival, a potentially attractive element for both business and leisure customers.

In a radiology service, "busy professional" patients may focus on waiting times, while the frail and elderly may focus on constant communication and timings that suit their lifestyle. An interview-based analysis of value features for a district hospital with elderly patients discovered the following points.

	Perception by frail/elderly users	Perception by organisation
Basic	Cost of car parking	Patients arrive in appropriate dress with correct information
	Treated with respect	
	Location of toilets	
	Length of wait	
Satisfying	Information about where they are in the process and what will happen next	The shorter the visit, the better
Attractive	Lunchtime appointment means that lunch can be eaten at the hospital restaurant, "a day out"	Information about where the patients are in the process and what happens next
	Appointment at the allocated time	

Table 3: Understanding different value drivers
for customers versus suppliers

As the table illustrates, the basic features valued by these customers can be implemented and the relevant benefit measured with little organisational change. Measurement of customer feedback and staff morale are likely to show improvement. As a consequence, the service could be adapted to accommodate this particular cohort before embarking on a large scale transformation. Organisations adept at making sure they address basic elements, and reduce dissatisfaction, may find that this leads to a reduction in other costs: for example, treating patients with respect will lead to fewer complaints and less staff stress/sickness and the organisation's reputation for service will improve.

Figure 5: Understanding expectations of patients in a hospital

The context for transformational change

Large-scale change programmes designed to deliver improvements in infrastructure or process, rather than products or services, should address the following questions around the value of change:

- What investment in the transformation will give the best returns in terms of perceived quality of service and satisfaction to internal customers and external stakeholders?

- Where do we need to manage customer expectations during and after the transformative change?

- Which elements of delivery/solutions need to be downgraded?

- Where should the focus be on staff training and behaviours?

CHAPTER 2
Systematic Clearing Out

An organisational clear-out of materials and information is important because it allows a person to be fully present and to think clearly about the task, rather than be distracted by information which is no longer relevant. Information retained by the subconscious, rather than being disposed of, can have a negative effect, as exemplified by the *Zeigarnik Theory.*

The Zeigarnik[6] theory states that people remember uncompleted or interrupted tasks better than those they have completed; the subconscious uses up energy thinking about unfinished tasks rather than anticipating the goal ahead or focusing on the present.

---

6 Bluma Zeigarnik, 'On Finished and Unfinished Tasks', in A Sourcebook of Gestalt Psychology, ed. by W. D. Ellis (New York: Humanities Press, 1967), pp. 300–314.

While clear-outs can be carried out regularly or at specific times, they must always have a specific purpose. Clear-outs can be used to:

1. Support decision-making
2. Start a new strategy
3. Review a project upon completion
4. Solve problems

Clear-outs to support decision-making

Clear-outs can be useful when decision-making processes are confused, acting as a spur to review current strategy or implementation based on past decisions. They can also help in implementing a decision that has already been made but not fully communicated, or lead to the discovery of evidence which resolves differences that have festered between departments or individuals.

Clear-outs at the launch of a new strategy

Organisations often decide on a change of direction, while staff continue to be guided by information, documents and knowledge based on old strategies. A good time for a clear-out is during the launch of a strategy or change of direction. A clear-out acts as a good check for finishing all previous project activities, to make sure there is space for thinking through and implementing a new strategy. A good time to do this is shortly after a launch, when it is useful to give time to teams within the organisation to archive material and ideas that are no longer relevant.

Clear-outs at the end of a project

A third opportunity occurs when a team has just achieved a major goal. A clear-out ensures the task has been completed, but it also ensures that people have time to tidy up loose ends, and organise knowledge and deliverables into relevant locations or storage so that they can move on. Many projects are finished with some incomplete documentation: this means later review or refinement is more difficult to carry out and acts as an energy drain on the subconscious. Belbin's "completer-finisher"[7] (i.e. a person who ties up loose ends at the completion of a piece of work) is the ideal person to head up the clear-out at the end of a project.

Clear-outs as a problem-solving mechanism

How often have we wasted time talking to people about information when the desired material is sitting on the bookshelf, or has already been covered in previous work? A clear-out is a perfect way of uncovering essential, hidden nuggets of information. People who move house often experience a moment when they discover something, once treasured but long forgotten, that could play an important role in their lives again. While looking through the old strategy material of one of my clients, I noticed a set of values that fully supported the attempts we were then making to create collaborative workspaces. Feeding those same values back to the directors sparked a terrific momentum in the project, as they recognised the strong link between the values and

---

7 R Meredith Belbin, Team Roles at Work, 2nd edition (Oxford: Butterworth-Heinemann Publications, 2010), p.22.

the current status of their work. This is supported by the *Serendipity Theory* of the "happy accident".

Figure 6: Getting lost in paper

Ikujiro Nonaka, an organisational theorist, points out that innovation has an element of serendipity, and links the success of Japanese companies to the subjective insights, intuitions and hunches of individual employees by making those insights available for testing and use by the company as a whole.

Untidiness affects our way of thinking. The broken window theory [see *Broken Windows Theory*] states that when people do not take care of things in their local environment, it leads to more disorganisation. Conversely, when the environment is ordered, people work to maintain that order. This is because the environment creates the social norm and people observe this unwritten rule.

Broken windows theory[8,9]

"When there are no, or few people around, individuals are forced to look for other clues, called signals, as to what the social norms allow them to do and how great the risk of getting caught is.

An ordered and clean environment sends the signal that this is a place which is monitored; people here conform to the common norms of non-criminal behaviour. A disordered environment which is littered, vandalised and not maintained sends the opposite signal: this is a place where people do as they please and where they get away with that, without being detected. As people tend to act the way they think others act, they are more likely to act "disorderly" in the disordered environment".[10]

There is one very simple question to ask during a clear-out: what can we stop doing now that does not benefit customers? Clear-outs can be used to archive or remove superseded paperwork, for example a printed report that no one uses or a procedure that no one follows anymore.

A tidy workplace does not have to mean a clinically sterile workplace: it is not about making automatons

8 Wilcox, P; Quisenberry, N; Cabrera, DT; Jones, S (2004), "Busy places & broken windows?: Toward Defining the Role of Physical Structure and Process in Community Crime Models", Sociological Quarterly 45 (2): 185–207.

9 Wilson, James Q; Kelling, George L (Mar 1982), "Broken Windows: The police and neighborhood safety", The Atlantic, March 1982

10 "Broken windows theory", adapted from Wikipedia, https://en.wikipedia.org/wiki/Broken_windows_theory [accessed 22 June 2015].

of people.[11] The purpose of removing objects and information is to de-clutter and give the mind space to focus on value added activities. Being "tidy" is not to do with an individual's habits: people have and will always have different ways of working. As long as it doesn't restrict flow, or create mixed messages, it is best to incorporate individual nuances.

Scheduled clear-outs

As well as intervention-based clear-outs described above, organisations should have a large-scale clear-out every six months, with well defined policies regarding criteria for the removal of outdated materials and information. This clear-out is a crucial part of the "Lean"[12] method invented by Toyota. The company has a 5S principle that encapsulates clear-outs. Although this method can be seen in manufacturing organisations, I have yet to find some functions where this is sustained in the service sector.

11 Black Tape Madness for tidy desks [HM Revenues and Customs – Lean Project], Metro Newspaper 4 January 2007.

12 Jeffrey Liker, 'The Toyota Way' (New York: McGraw Hill, 2004).

Figure 7: Planned regular clear-outs

What are the 5S's?

Sorting

Eliminate all unnecessary tools, parts, instructions and information. Go through all information, tools, materials, and specifics in work areas/IT systems. Keep essential items and keep them in accessible places. Discard everything else or store it if infrequently used.

Set in Order

"A place for everything and everything in its place". Make sure that all parts, information and materials are in the right place, are visual and are organised in the order of use.

Shine/Secure

Keep the workplace tidy, organised and secure. At the end of each period of work leave the place "as you find it". Everyone then knows that everything is where it belongs. Maintaining cleanliness and order should be part of the daily work, not an occasional activity initiated when things get too messy.

We also need to consider "electronic" clear-outs of information on personal computers and network servers. Shared drives quickly get cluttered with outdated project information. This may be because there are no rules on how and when to delete unwanted material for fear of destroying something valuable. Many companies suffer from replication of data and archived information which is not properly referenced or is unsecured.

A knowledge manager (a role which should be created if it doesn't yet exist) can act as the clear-out co-ordinator – the one who ensures that there is a "drumbeat" of clear-outs, and that any new, undiscovered knowledge is properly archived, referenced or brought to the attention of the right person.

Standardise

This is a way to create a standard procedure/process for the three elements above, so that it is followed on a regular basis, e.g at the start of the day.

Sustain

Sustain is all about management commitment to maintain the first 4S's so that it is embedded as part of a culture in an organisation.

How to approach a clear-out

So what are the ground rules during the process of clear-out?

The company could decide to stop activity – "down tools" where possible – or get cover from another department. It is important that teams carry out the sorting and clearing together, rather than as individuals. The group then shares the workload which can create an infectious energy to build momentum and allow the power of serendipity. Make the clear-out exciting and dynamic: combine it with a social or fun element, like a dress down day. Departments could have scheduled arrangements where they cover each other's activities for events such as a clear-out day.

A clear-out day could be created with a specific agenda. For example a ninety-minute staff meeting, run by the staff rather than managers, and a team lunch followed by a clear-out and rationalisation for the rest of the day:

a   The initial stage might involve small teams who examine materials and flag (red tags are useful) items which are unused or rarely used.

b   This could be followed by a "town hall meeting" where the treatment of the red-tagged materials would be agreed upon.

c   Based on the agreements from the meeting, materials could be tagged further where necessary. For example, materials to be disposed of in the future could be tagged with a disposal date and given to facilities to store and eventually dispose of, or all policies could be modified to include details of the retaining period for all documents.

People can be encouraged to use the clear-out to find "knowledge nuggets", those hidden bits of information which could be useful, with a tally kept of who discovers the most knowledge nuggets. This process closely links to that of serendipity, finding useful things without actually looking for them.

People can organise their information into virtual waste-baskets and knowledge baskets: anything labelled "waste" should be stored for six months, then deleted. Knowledge that might prove useful in the future should be logged and put into a relevant database. The purge extends to emails, shared folders and even internal communications areas, such as the intranet. Most formal, legal and finance papers only need to be retained for a set number of years. A company retention policy should cover those.

Organisations' memories need to be preserved, but learning to let go of both physical and electronic material is also important. A regular purge of unnecessary materials renews mental energy and allows organisations to look to the future. Regular clear-outs lift the spirit, embed real knowledge and allow an organisation to let go.

While clear-outs can go too far and get rid of useful information, a "hoarder" will always use this argument as an excuse for inaction. A clear retention policy will negate this effect.

In summary, frequently, people resist change by saying, "I'm too busy doing my important job to get involved in tidying up". Often the benefits, such as a post clear-out "good" feeling and having the correct information easily to hand, are not properly communicated. One way to avoid this is to have a clear-out policy with a top-down mandate. Another is to use other forms of energy (provision of snacks or other treats, for example) to start the momentum. At the end of the process there should be a review of benefits, such as useful documents found that were once lost, but also building team relationships from the positive emotional feeling of clearing out.

CHAPTER 3
Continuous Review

Many organisations are more like an oil tanker, which is difficult to manoeuvre once set on a course, than an ant, which meanders constantly to find its target.

In most organisations, review is carried out from the top down, driven by a study of external outlook, forecast and previous organisational performance. This informs annual decisions about improving business processes which are cascaded down to all employees.

This approach creates lag between decision-making and actual change or implementation. When reality meets theory, often the change isn't implemented in the way envisaged. There can be several reasons including: staff resistance to change, the basic impracticality of the change envisioned, a lack of capability in the organisation to work in a systematic way to make change happen, or a lack of effective leadership to build the right momentum.

An entire organisation needs to be in a state of review, not just annually but continuously, to enable it to move rapidly while overcoming hurdles. Change can only start from awareness and understanding, and a process of continuous review can help create the momentum for change. Continuous review is also the building block that makes an organisation more adaptable and likely to deal with external threats even when they are not anticipated.

Figure 8: Small cracks may not withstand external shock

Review is difficult for many people: when things appear to be working well, the question is: "If it isn't broken, why try to fix it?" However, without rigorous review, there will be instances where minor issues are missed resulting in small cracks that cannot withstand external shock as shown in Figure 8. Take, for example, the failure of a large hospital, the Mid Staffordshire Hospital in the UK, which led to a full public enquiry and had to be eventually reconfigured.[13] There were a host of failures, but the report noted that the impact of failure was partly led by an "assumption that monitoring performance

13 Report of Mid Staffordshire NHS Foundation Trust Public Enquiry, chaired by Robert Francis, (London: The Stationary Office, 2013).

management or intervention was the responsibility of someone else". It also noted that standards devised at the hospital were top-down, not bottom-up, and were driven by bureaucracy rather than what mattered to patients.

What we need to understand about reviews

Sometimes continuous improvement initiatives are disbanded due to a lack of momentum once they achieve a particular, often artificial, target based on a one-off project. Continuous review should be more than meeting a goal: it ought to be a constant review of the organisation's current practices, in light of the business's aims and strategy.

There are several stages to continuous review. Each should be carried out on a "drumbeat" basis: daily, weekly, monthly and quarterly.

Daily

So what happens in a daily review? The questions should allow a fast flow of energy. A "stand-up" or open meeting space helps keep things brief. The sessions should be no longer than fifteen minutes, with no more than four questions, focused around issue management and assurance.

Figure 9: The daily review

The question about unexpected events points to process issues either brought about by a common cause (e.g. a procedure was missed yesterday) or a special cause (e.g. the snow caused us to start work late). All causes need to be acknowledged and suggestions for process improvement and risk management need to be pointed out.

This process of review gives a full bottom-up view of the day's issues which within two hours can be fully escalated through to the very top of the organisation. This process is about solving today's problem today, stopping it from escalating and providing an early warning signal about potential danger ahead.

In some organisations actions are recorded in an email during the review and sent instantly on completion of the meeting. Problems are only escalated if they are beyond the control of the local team and create an obstacle in carrying out that day's work.

Figure 10: Reviews identify a common view of problems

Snapshot of a review

Daily reviews should work across the whole organisation. A large shipbuilding company employing over two thousand people in buildings across disparate sites used the following sequence each morning:

- 07:30 Shop floor review
- 08:00 First line management review
- 08:30 Middle management review
- 09:00 Senior management review

In addition, we can have weekly reviews with questions based around the improvement of the operational processes.

Weekly

Weekly reviews involve more of an overview of the activity. They point out where things can be improved across a process in which a team works:

- What's working well? (Can we do more of this?)
- What can we stop doing that provides no real value?
- What have we learnt this week?

The "what's working well" question is critical, as it uses positive energy and experience to improve or leverage a process or model that works well. In any organisation where I have been brought in to look at process issues, this is an area of questioning I always ask, as the solutions to problems can often emanate from the processes that are already good. Appreciative Inquiry[14] is a concept that uses positivity and working with the "best of what is".

A hospital trust in the Midlands asked: "What can we stop doing that provides no real value to our patients?" They studied their outpatient X-ray appointments and found that booked appointments created overhead costs in the number of "did not attend" and the administrative process. The system also provided little value to patients: most injuries and illnesses needed swift diagnosis. The patients just wanted to be seen as quickly as possible and were open to new approaches provided they did not have to wait. A walk-in system that was both less costly and provided better value to

---

14 Shaked, David. Strength-based lean six sigma: building positive and engaging business improvement. London England: Kogan Page, 2014. Print.

patients was implemented easily once a demand and capacity analysis was carried out. The system proved so successful that it prompted one patient to write to the local newspaper with their positive experience!

Running like clockwork

SIR – Is this a record?

I had an appointment with my GP in Harrold at 9.20am.

He sent me for a chest X-ray. At 10.26am I took the bus to Bedford arriving at 11am.

I immediately transferred to a bus taking me to Bedford hospital where I arrived at 11.20am.

At 11.22am I walked into the X-ray department, 11.23am summoned in to X-ray room, 11.26am all done, 11.35am catch back bus back to bus station. Noon catch bus back to Harrold. Brill!

Please do not slag off the NHS and Stagecoach, both were brilliant.

Edgar W. Stock
Harrold

Figure 11: Letter in local newspaper

Monthly

The questions here are more based around direction and should typically take no more than two hours.

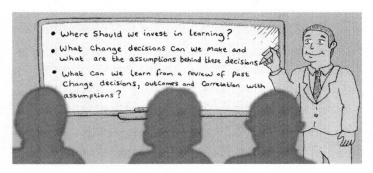

Figure 12: Holding a monthly review

The monthly meeting is a critical meeting as it is here that decisions about change are made. It is time to reflect on areas that need improvement. More important is to note the assumptions behind these decisions. A review of these assumptions will help with assessing the outcome in a robust way.

The element of decisions and assumptions can easily be recorded on a simple matrix; typically each team should have such a log.

Study on assumptions and decisions: Olympics 2012

It was assumed that the Olympics would generate higher volume in retail sales.[15] The original forecast of growth in retail sales being 3.5%.[16]

The main assumptions were that there would be more visitors and they would buy goods and services during their visit. In particular, the longer opening hours during the Olympics would have an impact.

In reality retail sales in the UK were lower in August as the popularity of the Olympics hit traffic at stores, a survey has shown.[17] In addition, sales in the London's West End were 4.6% lower during the Olympics period.[18]

There were two factors involved: people who congregated around the Olympic village and venues having spent a large sum on tickets, did not have any extra cash to spend; local Britons were absorbed by watching the Olympics on television: ninety percent

---

15 Karen McCandless, "London 2012 Olympics Impact on Retail,' OnWindows, 4 April 2012, http://www.onwindows.com/Articles/London–2012-Olympics-impact-on-retail/6701/Default.aspx [accessed 5 June 2015]

16 "Olympic year to drive 3.5% increase in retail sales growth in London's West End," The Retail Bulletin, 16 January 2012, http://www.theretailbulletin.com/news/olympic_year_to_drive_35_increase_in_retail_sales_growth_in_londons_west_end_16-01-12/ [accessed 2 June 2015]

17 "Retail sales 'hurt by Olympics' in August," BBC, 4 September 2012, http://www.bbc.co.uk/news/business-19468578 [accessed 5 June 2014]

18 "London's West End: Review and Outlook," (Chicago: Jones Lang Lasalle IP Inc., 2013) http://holtest.web.coop/wp-content/uploads/2013/01/West-End-Tracker-2013.pdf [accessed 2 June 2015] p.15.

watched it every day[19] and spent less time outside the home, including shopping. Clearly the assumption turned out to be wrong and the lessons learnt were about the ways in which people make a choice between enjoyment from viewing a special event versus shopping, rather than doing both.

Retail sales fell 0.4% on a like-for-like basis in the month of the Olympics compared to the same month the year before, according to the British Retail Consortium (BRC). Excluding Easter, it was the weakest month since November. "The feel good factor from the Olympics failed to inspire spending", the BRC said. In particular, online shopping grew 4.8% in August, the lowest increase since the BRC started collecting the data in October 2008. "There's no evidence here of any Olympic boost to retail sales overall", said BRC director general, Stephen Robertson. "Hot weather and the Olympics did help sales of party food and drink but that was more than offset by a really weak performance for non-food goods".

Quarterly

The questions here are about investment.

- What have we achieved?
- How are our long-term initiatives progressing?
- Where do we need to invest in capability and capacity?
- What governance and assurance do we need to improve?

19 "London 2012 Olympics deliver record viewing figures for BBC," BBC, 13 August 2012, http://www.bbc.co.uk/mediacentre/latestnews/2012/olympic-viewing-figs.html [accessed 5 June 2014]

All organisations have yearly reviews. This is a strategic decision based on the external environment and customer needs. Michael E Porter talks of Five Forces[20] which create a set of assumptions for the organisation. Strategic changes, such as investing in a new service line or product, or a divestment, are separate activities and not included in a continuous review of ongoing activities.

"Subsidiarity" means performing tasks at the lowest, most local and practical level in large governments. A similar concept should exist in large organisations, so that decisions and knowledge are encouraged down to the lowest possible relevant level. The review process itself creates a sense of ownership of problems and improvement becomes a self-fulfilling, virtuous circle. Senior management often articulate frustration at the lack of decision-making and ownership at lower levels, but it is often the organisational system that thwarts this subsidiarity. They are quick to point to poor decision-making in the organisation after the event, but the real reason lies in the process of decision-making and review that they have failed to create at the right levels. A hierarchical structure is often used to force decision-making down the chain and the excuse of 'poor execution' used to protect each layer of management from the failure that occurs "underneath". This is the most common complaint from people in public sector organisations: they don't get a chance to be involved in decision-making that impacts. An Ipsos MORI poll found forty-eight percent of people would like to be

20 Michael E. Porter, Competitive Strategy: Techniques for Analysing Industries and Competitors, (New York: Free Press, 1980).

involved in local decision-making for public services delivered locally.[21]

Some organisations talk about "allowing decisions to be made lower down", but do not have a structure to facilitate this. Without one, it is just wishful thinking. People at the bottom are also afraid of making mistakes: they will be the ones who carry the blame.

In large-scale transformation programmes, continuous review provides a drumbeat for improvement, without creating bureaucratic overhead, making transformative change much easier to put into practice.

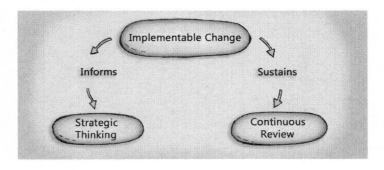

Figure 13: Linking strategy to continuous review

In summary, continuous review becomes the cornerstone for an organisation to be in "flow" in the face of challenges, rather than to "barge through". When an organisation is going through transformative change, it makes the process of implementation easier.

In many organisations, hierarchical planning and top-down review has taken over from setting up the right

21 Ipsos MORI, "What do people want, need, and expect from public services?" (London: 2020 Public Services Trust at the RSA, 2010).

mechanism of review when implementing large-scale change.

Continuous review differs from continuous improvement. The latter focuses on improvement and action while continuous review concentrates on awareness and a full understanding of the implications of any actions.

CHAPTER 4
RACI

Introduction

This chapter is about RACI (Responsibility, Account-ability, Consultation and Information), a manage-ment tool which is extremely useful as an enabler in deciding "who does what" at different hierarchies of decision-making/activities.

RACI can clarify the organisational decision-making framework for transformational change, by allocating responsibilities, identified at each stage or level to teams or individuals, rather than being retained at the very top. The fail-safe device is that senior management is consulted either at critical or pre-agreed moments.

Dealing with complex transformational change requires clear thought processes, structures, work and project streams, and accountability from the outset. Each change team needs to be empowered to make appropriate decisions so that the team can self-regulate without needing to refer to others continuously while delivering effective, actionable results.

In large-scale transformation programmes it is almost impossible to monitor each aspect in detail. Trying to do so can itself inhibit the process of change: keeping records takes time and presents a picture that seldom reflects what is actually happening. In fact, detailed monitoring of any complex change from the top down puts the focus of motivation into monitoring and away from creating the momentum needed for transformational change. Individuals and groups at all levels of the process need to be motivated to deliver complex change.

Paradoxically, the more complex the change, the less detailed information is required from each level or group. The essentials to manage complexity are better quality decision-making and the ability to manage ambiguity. This enables each sub-division of the overall process to be in control, and to keep others informed, motivated and up to date.

There are numerous examples of change initiatives that have failed, taken far longer than necessary or created more problems than envisaged. This is not due to capacity or capability issues. Primarily, it is due to a lack of proper structure around roles assigned to projects or activities. One example is the £12.4 billion NHS "Connecting for Health" project, which failed to meet its objectives. The core reason was the lack of bottom-up accountability for the programme. Martyn Hart, Chairman of the National Outsourcing Association[22] stated: "Maybe they should have eaten this elephant in small chunks. That would be better for

22 Oats, John. "NHS IT: what went wrong, what will go wrong". http://www.theregister.co.uk/2008/05/30/nhs_it_analysis/print.html 30 May 2008. Web. January 2015.

smaller, local businesses... It's a blame culture and a question of check lists – you're safe if all the boxes are ticked, even if it doesn't make any sense. There's a pressure to conform – it is very difficult to stand up and say no".

Problems in complex change occur most often when decision-making becomes complicated due to the number of players and factors involved. Add to this a lack of clarity in accountability and the outcome is that issues and problems are missed. Assessing what has gone wrong fosters a blame culture. Common symptoms include too little or too much communication: the extremes of either "no one told me about that" or "I'm drowning in emails".

Many organisations begin with the intention of making decisions at each level. However the uncertainty and insecurity people face in large, complex organisations mean they often prefer someone "up there" to make the decisions. This invariably leads to delays, as well as people unwilling to take risks. More importantly, it leads to an exponential growth in unnecessary communications: issues and information are filtered up, and decisions or requests for more information are filtered down. This creates over involvement, or no involvement. "Over involvement" is where people are seemingly involved in a piece of work where they have no input. "No involvement" is where people are not even asked for their view in an area where they feel entitled to an input and their views are likely to be of value. In this scenario, senior management is keen to be seen to be making the key decisions and thus appearing to be in control. In my experience, the more decisions one person has to take around a complex process, the less likely the process is to deliver anything.

Using RACI

Figure 14: RACI: Defining who does what

At its simplest, RACI stands for the four roles people could be involved in for any activity:

R = Responsibility   Makes the change happen, delivers the work

A = Accountability   Ensures work gets completed, provides resources

C = Consultation   Is consulted about the task or activity but does not get directly involved

I = Information Needs to know when
a decision or action
has been taken

The Responsibility role is allocated to those who do the work. That is, those who add value to the delivery. In RACI, one or more people can be assigned to delivery.

The Accountability role is assigned to the person who is accountable for the ultimate outcome of the work. This person, whose "neck is on the line", may also have responsibility for all or some of the work. Experience shows that people welcome taking accountability if they feel that they have the tools to succeed.

A critical factor in complex transformations is the need for clear differentiation between responsibility and accountability.

The Consultation role is for those who need to be consulted as part of the activity. One thing many organisations are weak in is the ability to recognise when it is necessary to consult an expert without giving away responsibility for delivery. People often resist involving others, concerned that it will lead to delay, force weaknesses to be revealed or result in advice which doesn't suit the leader's style. History is littered with mistakes made due to lack of adequate consultation with the right stakeholders.

The Information role identifies the individuals who need to be informed after a decision or action is taken. This informs those affected by change and is critical in transformation. Clarity on who does and doesn't need to be informed is essential to prevent over-communication and to make messages directly relevant to the recipient. A single way of communicating (e.g. mail shots) may appear to be a good strategy, but might not work. For example, a mail shot might be sent: it could then appear that everyone has been informed, but the message might not have been read. For any family who has moved home, RACI will be a very practical reminder of defining who does what, as all activities need clear allocation of roles and commitment for a successful move.

Figure 15: Roles and activities in moving home

Overall A = Operations Director						
Activity/ Role	Sales	Planning	Technical	Business Analyst	Support Staff	Project Support
Confirm Require- ments	A/R	R	I	I	-	-
Plan Capacity	C	A/R	R	-	I	R
Techni- cal Design	I	-	A/R	R		I
Test	I	I	R	C	I	A
Sign off	A/R	I	R	-	I	R

Table 4: A simple RACI for delivering a technical product

The example above shows how accountability for tasks has been shared by all stakeholders. In many situations one person is "in charge" of all of the activites, which can lead to strained relationships, or worse! The deliberate spreading of accountability is an important good practice when using the RACI tool. From the example above, even though the technical team carries out the design work, accountability lies with sales to ensure that it meets customer expectations at sign off. It also shows very clearly which stakeholders are consulted or informed, ensuring that there is no communication overload. The Operations Director is accountable for the process, ensuring that the right resources and roles are allocated to both deliver the work and for effective decision-making.

How to develop a RACI

The RACI tool should be used in a collaborative setting, with visual grids and sticky notes. When teams first meet, prior to any agreement on "who is doing what", the RACI tool focuses the debate and provides clarity. Most importantly, it ensures people understand what activities they are not involved in.

All teams developing a RACI approach should:

1. Be clear about the purpose or goal of the project and its deliverables;

2. Identify key activities (at a high level);

3. Identify key roles but not necessarily assigning people to roles straight away.

It may be that one person takes on two different roles in a specific programme or that one role is shared.

Step 1 – Gather team and agree purpose

Roles and activities are written on sticky notes and displayed on a grid for all to see, followed by a debate on the allocation of RACI across all activities. If the team strengths are not well understood, it is likely that a skills list or a Belbin[23] type analysis needs to be carried out first.

Step 2 – Build first stage of RACI and reflect

This step allows further review and analysis. The person with overall accountability may consult with people

23 Belbin, R. M Team roles at work. Oxford: Butterworth-Heinemann, 2010.

outside the team. Individuals should be canvassed to ensure that they are comfortable in their role.

Step 3 – Formalise RACI and analyse

The RACI concept is very useful where there are cross-functional or cross-organisational teams. For example, the UK public body, Network Rail, uses RACI at many of its depots, where there are both a combination of different staff trades and a host of external specialist contractors.

The RACI approach provides a framework for working – it does not replace deeper dialogue or discussion, and does not foster management control. RACI provides the freedom to act with creativity and teamwork, to help deliver results; it is not a substitute for leadership.

An ongoing review of RACI is significant and will form part of the continuous review of an overall project or array of activities. RACI also helps with the reorganisation of teams, should this become necessary (see Chapter 5). It often provides evidence that changes within a team are required.

We will look at two examples of how a review and analysis of an ongoing RACI chart can indicate the need for changes. Both are to do with transformational programme activities.

Overall A = Board Director	Pro-gramme Director	Pro-gramme Support Manager	Busi-ness Cham-pion A	Busi-ness Cham-pion B	Board Direc-tor
Benefits Case	A/R	I	I	I	C
Benefit Mapping	A/R	R	C		C
Transfor-mational Plan	A/R	-	C	C	C
Prog ramme Support Office	A/R	R	I	I	I
Prog ramme Launch	A/R	R	I	I	I

Table 5: Analysing a completed RACI chart

In the example shown, the board director has overall accountability and the programme director is accountable for all the activities.

If one person has too many accountability roles they are likely to be swamped in decision-making. This has several dangers: the risk of burnout for the individual; the whole process becoming a tick-box exercise; risk avoidance.

If no one is willing to take on accountability, this raises a critical issue. Is the activity too complex? Should it be broken down into sub-activities? Does it carry a high risk, and if so why? There can be a tendency for people, during the high energy of a workshop, to take on accountability for which, with hindsight, they have no influence or expertise. So a period of reflection and validation of accountabilities is important.

For creating a RACI, a team approach works best. For RACI to be of value, activities should be at a level that requires thought and detail in design or delivery. This will mean better spread of accountability and responsibility with improved quality of work and better handover between streams of work.

The lack of an organising tool such as RACI can have devastating consequences. The banking crisis of 2008 is a good example where there was no clear overall accountability for banking governance in the UK. The banks assumed the FSA had final accountability, the FSA assumed that banks were self-regulating, and the Bank of England assumed that it had to set macro targets without properly considering underlying processes.

Overall Accountability = Director	Role 1	Role 2	Role 3	Role 4	Role 5
Design of Solution	A/R	R	R	R	R
Stakeholder Management	R	R	A/R	R	R
Training	R	C	C	C	A/R
Prototype	R	A/R	R	R	R
Implement Process Change	A/R	A/R	R	R	C

Table 6: Analysing a completed RACI chart

Let's consider the example in the table above which may be suitable in some situations. It raises the important question of whether it is appropriate that most roles are involved in responsibility or consultation for all activities. This indicates that decision-making will be slow because everyone is involved in several activities, or has been asked to do too much. In some highly complex tasks this may be necessary, but it is more likely that the person who is accountable overall is trying to gain extra assurance from others, or that certain team members themselves are not willing, or have not been given the opportunity, to take greater responsibility. Therefore, their perception is that they need to get everyone involved in everything.

The activity 'Implement Process Change', is a good example of where two people have decided to take on "joint accountability". Maybe they enjoyed working together or felt they needed to share what is seen as a high-risk activity. Even though the idea seems good, it must be avoided. Joint responsibility, yes; joint accountability, no. Joint accountability wipes out the key elements of individual empowerment and ownership, which are important as the project progresses.

How RACI helps transformation and change

It is commonly accepted that the best way to sustain change is by allowing decision-making to take place at the level of competence nearest to those affected by its outcome (i.e. subsidiarity) or from the bottom up. In this way, decisions are likely to take account of the realities of any situation.

RACI is a living tool: roles and responsibility change over time. As a project workstream develops, roles need to change, as do responsibilities. The RACI chart should be adapted at key review points. It is critical that the RACI is visual and can be seen by all participants, and it is important that the RACI chart is used as a way of challenging those who have mismatched ownership with respect to their roles.

Sometimes third parties need to be involved in change projects or in delivering a service. This often means accountability to deliver can be misplaced. RACI is a good way to ensure accountability exists within the organisation boundary, but responsibility exists with the third party.

RACI is a powerful tool to use for continuous review (see Chapter 3). During continuous review, RACI affords insight into how different teams have performed in their roles. This in turn provides valuable learning prospects.

In a complex programme, multiple RACI charts can exist, or a number of RACIs can be joined up to form a "mega RACI".

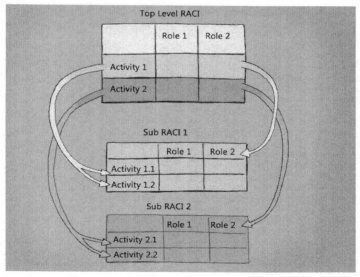

Figure 16: RACI drill down

When several workstream RACIs lead to a "mega RACI", it clarifies the ways in which different accountabilities are tied to the overall programme. This ensures a true cascade of accountabilities. It also ensures that accountability is at the appropriate level in a large transformation programme. Hence the term "the buck stops here" applies to the accountable person at each level.

When not to use RACI

Leaders of change processes need to acknowledge that using the RACI tool also means "letting go" of making decisions in every aspect within the organisation.

RACI will not work in an environment where the required levels of competence to carry out tasks, or a need for subsidiarity, do not exist. It also will not work if management attempt to use the tool to ensure accountability and drive change, but in practice still control the detail of the work and want to steer all decision-making. In that situation, the use of RACI becomes a "smoke screen" designed to persuade others that there is shared decision-making where there is not. In such a case the RACI chart has little value or purpose.

The checks and balances built into the RACI process are the surest guarantee of success and provide assurance to leaders who are task driven and prone to interfering.

Some organisations have tried to introduce greater control from the top with, for example, a RACIV where the "V" stands for "veto". This gives someone at senior management level the power of veto if they feel the decision reached will cause systematic imbalance. This is self-defeating. The veto power undermines decision-making and increases the likelihood of decisions that will create an imbalance, as decisions made will be based on the "fear of a veto". The use of a hierarchal RACI tree of accountability is a better, and more effective, way of managing conflict.

RACI works effectively when the purpose of the overall project is well understood and accepted. In some cases the purpose is not understood, but the team members following RACI, work blindly because of extrinsic motivation. They will invariably produce poor results, although they doubtlessly work very hard. This is a major cause of demotivation and disillusionment among staff.

The RACI tool does not necessarily drive the quality of work. It is the responsibility of the person with overall accountability to ensure that the real value of the work is accepted and understood, and that this is clear before any activities are embarked upon. In short, a prerequisite for RACI is to ensure that the purpose or goal of the project, and its deliverables, are clear before resources and tasks are organised.

In summary the RACI tool aligns decision-making with activities. The aim of this chapter has been to demonstrate that the RACI tool allows a team based approach in connecting decision-making roles and activities around a change project. It also shows communication channels in an easy-to-use matrix. This gives flexibility with control and decision-making with accountability. The organisation gains the freedom to manage a variety of tasks and projects with subsidiarity and a focus on the quality of the work.

CHAPTER 5
Creating and Dismantling
High Performance Teams

This chapter is about the creation of high-performing, "on-the-ground" teams, which are essential ingredients to manage the constant change that businesses face today.

Teams are at the core of any business. However, when they do not work, teams are also a source of trouble. Although businesses may have good strategic cases for change, they need to bear in mind that teams which fail make a direct contribution to change programmes, which can then result in poor implementation or lack of sustainability. Complex organisations, more than most, need not just good teams, but high-performing teams that deliver exceptional performance.

Figure 17: Creating a successful team

Successful teams come with a hazard of their own: they must be disbanded at the right time. This is one of the hardest things to do when teams work well. Success can only be guaranteed in times of change when the team members' purpose and motivation remain unchanged; this is unlikely as the organisation's environment is always evolving.

Why high performance teams?

Management in organisations have become very slick at developing grand strategies. However, there is never enough consideration of the people on the ground who will deliver that strategy. In complex organisations, support functions develop their own agenda; they often become inward-looking and functionally competitive, losing touch with the customers' needs. The real value of strategy can only come from the people who intrinsically understand, from training and experience, whether the new strategy will make a real difference to the customer or make their work meaningful. The effort required to implement change, making it practical, applicable and sustainable, is seemingly formidable – this is the reason why in many cases the benefits of strategies, articulated and well-reasoned on paper, are never delivered.

What is a high performance team?

High performance teams (HPTs) implement and sustain complex change. These teams not only achieve focused goals; they create an environment that is open to change and learning, enabling flexibility and realisation of strategy.

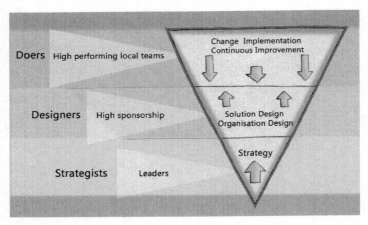

Figure 18: High performing local teams make change sustainable

High performance teams are extremely creative and innovative, with high aspirations. The Australian cricket team, for example, has experimented with ambidextrous players and recently hired a baseball coach to see if this could assist the players' game. The team clearly have aspirations beyond their present level of excellence.

So how do we create such a team and what are its characteristics? Whenever I ask anyone about the best team that they have worked in (whether professionally or otherwise), the responses are similar:

- 'Fun!'
- 'Exciting!'
- 'Everyone is self-motivated.'
- 'We wanted to deliver.'
- 'We used to dream of success.'
- 'It felt like the team members were my best friends.'
- 'We delivered more than we initially expected.'
- 'Some fantastic ideas.'
- 'We were all leaders.'
- 'We were aware of how well we were doing.'

The members of a theatre production team are a good example of a HPT; although individual roles are defined, prompt feedback and mutual respect is essential if the group is to deliver excellence night after night. So, for example, people in theatre often talk about success in the terms quoted above.

"Mind the Gap" is a twenty-five-year-old organisation that brings together learning-disabled and non-disabled people to develop, exchange ideas and bring theatre productions together. This is a great example of a high performance team working with people of different abilities.

A developed "inner will" operating as a cross-functional group is a good starting definition of a high performing team. HPTs in areas of high interaction with customers or complex business processes are essential for a business within operational processes.

How to create a high performance team

Whether it be winning a trophy in sport, making a product or solving specific business process problems, all the experts agree that effective HPTs need to have focused, timed challenges which produce sustainable results. Having the right mix of talent, aptitude and ability is vital, and there must be genuine respect within the team for the skills, abilities and strengths that each brings, as well as acceptance of any individual shortcomings.

There has to be a sense of ownership of the team's shared goal or goals, as well as individual accountability in areas of specialist expertise, and members who take the initiative to ask for support or help if required.

Clive Woodward, ex-England rugby coach, stated in 2003 that "getting the right people is the biggest trick in business, and if you get one wrong coach in there it can take you a long time to sort out". The selection of a coach is a crucial decision; it could be someone from the organisation (such as a change-agent or a well-respected individual) or, for a short period, someone external who can bring fresh ideas with an objective point of view.

Hewlett Packard is a good example where coaching has been practised successfully for decades. One employee explained how his manager executed the HP technique:[24] "He only put in his oar when the project was on the line. Then he'd make some comments, guiding us in a direction. When the direction was established, he stepped away".

It is important that the team agrees from the beginning how to run meetings, the scope of the problems they are going to tackle and any ground rules. For example, at Network Rail, the employees at the depots who undertook change management training agreed working times and their commitment, from which they created team ground rules.

GROUND RULES
Mobiles on silent
All questions are good questions
Freedom to fail and learn from failure
Arrive on time
Have fun!

Table 7: Example of ground rules

These ground rules establish a fair and disciplined way of working and give members clarity about the boundaries within which the team operates. The example above is a sample of ground rules, but it should be stressed that each team should agree their own.

High performance teams thrive when they continue to learn, and to welcome and even embrace change. At Avon Cosmetics, it is the management's job to encour-

24 Jocelyn Dong, "The Rise and Fall of the HP Way", Palo Alto Way Weekly, 10 April 2002, http://www.paloaltoonline.com/weekly/morgue/2002/2002_04_10.hpway10.html [accessed 5 June 2014].

age learning in areas that have no direct link with the cosmetic business; Avon has recognised that the best way to retain their staff is to help them fulfil their individual motivations.

A HPT is not afraid to make decisions and act upon them. Sir Alex Ferguson, the lauded coach of Manchester United Football team, was famous for making decisions that, although sometimes unpopular, helped him create five different winning teams in his tenure.[25]

In the Mars Pathfinder programme, the idea of "decision-making on demand" was used. Project Manager Brian Muirhead states, "Rapid decision-making was a hallmark of our implementation of the Mars Pathfinder mission. The leadership had a deep knowledge of what was going on, so when problems arose we could fix them quickly and move on".[26] The team created a process, not to solidify decision-making, but to help everyone to move forward to a better understanding of the actual reality as it occurred.

25 Gary Curneen, "Coaching lessons from Sir Alex Ferguson", 10 May 2013 http://garycurneen.com/archives/1994 [accessed 5 June 2014].

26 Brian Muirhead, National Instrument Keynote Address, 15 August 2003. http://www.businesswire.com/news/home/20030815005241/en/Mars-Pathfinder-Leader-Delivers-Keynote-NIWeek-2003#.U5Bq93JdWSo [accessed 5 June 2014].

Figure 19: High performing teams reach new heights

High performance teams create and hone an inner desire for success. This is often reflected in the fun and humour, both very important ingredients, common in such teams. This leads to a relaxed environment which triggers creative ideas. During a coaching workshop, I set up teams to run goal-setting exercises, such as building paper towers or dealing with a desert-survival game, in order to engage the participants' lateral thinking skills. This focus and relaxation unveiled team abilities and characteristics which members did not know they had! I have seen team members from senior directors to shop-floor workers thrive on the challenge of working with each other. In displaying their creativity, they have become so absorbed in their common goal that they have forgotten any differences in status for the duration of the session.

> "A high performance workplace can expect to achieve a twenty-percent increase in productivity and profitability".
>
> Chartered Institute of Personnel, November 2003

Methods to understand team emotions

How often do you find teams using personalised methods or gut instincts to respond to a problem? A process that encompasses all aspects of a problem is not followed; there is no common way of working which would ensure that misunderstandings could not occur. There are many ways of problem-solving, including Shewhart's Plan-Do-Check-Act Cycle[27], a simple and cyclical way of making change that is based on using hypothesis, experiment and evaluation to get to an optimal outcome.

Being aware of these tools and their necessary methodologies makes the language of problem-solving common and systematic; when confronted with a performance challenge, the team can dig into their common toolkit and follow the process to its solution together.

There are several ways of assessing how a team is performing and what stage they have reached.

---

27 Walter Andrew Shewhart, Economic Control of Quality of Manufactured Product, Volume 509, (Wisconsin: Quality Press, 1980).

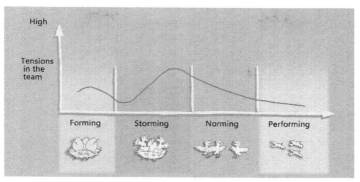

Figure 20: The cycle of team creation[28]

Many of the characteristics of HPTs do not arise naturally. A cycle must be completed before a team begins to perform. After the team is formed, "storming" needs to occur: this is when a real heart-to-heart about specific issues and ways of working takes place. Unless "storming" occurs, the team never performs. This is obvious in sport: the progress of Manchester United Football team or the English rugby team is highest when they have all been through a "storming" period. It is clear from Manchester United's approach that these storms are frequent, and even engineered to help create high performance without destroying morale. The trick for high performance teams is to get through this "storming" cycle quickly. Only after this can the team start performing.

Table 8 shows the difference between a HPT and a normal team. This is a good measure of assessing the nature of a team: the next time you see a group of people assembled to agree a strategy or solve a

28 Tuckman, Bruce W., Developmental sequence in small groups, (APA: Psychological Bulletin, Vol 63(6), 1965), page 384-399.

problem, ask yourself whether or not they are a high performance team.

	Team	High performance team
Leadership	Single leader	Shared leadership
Ownership	Individual	Mutual
Purpose	Specific	Highly focused
Development	Some	Continuous development
Meetings	'Let's discuss a problem.'	'Let's make decisions and act on them.'
Relationships	Good	Strong and deep
Aspiration	More than sum of individuals	Beyond expectation
Size	Varies	<8

Table 8: Differences between a normal team and a HPT
(adapted from article in Harvard Business Review[29])

High performance teams need the right balance of emotions in their members. Examples of key roles are given in Table 9. Every member has traits that contribute to the team but the important thing is to have balance – a HPT is going to be short-lived if it has too many "Plant" roles or is without an "Implementer". In his book Good to Great, Jim Collins says: "To build a successful organisation and team, you must get the right people on the bus". His research shows that profitable companies do this.

---

29 Katzenbach, Jon R.; Smith, Douglas K., The Discipline of Teams, (Harvard Business Review. Mar/Apr93, Vol. 71 Issue 2), page 111-120

They get the right people in the organisation first and then decide on the destination.

Role	Traits
Co-ordinator	'Let's get everyone together.'
Shaper	'Let's do it in this way.'
Implementer	'I am going to make this happen.'
Completer	'I must finish this task.'
Monitor/ Evaluator	'We are falling behind.'
Team Worker	'If the team wants it, I'll do it.'
Plant	'What if we changed direction?'
Resource Investigator	'I know someone who knows...'

Table 9: Adapted Belbin[30] model of eight key drivers of people

Dismantling a high performance team

Once a team does become successful, a more thorough analysis of the framework needs to be carried out to consider what should be kept and what should be changed. The very behaviours and attitudes that gave individuals the inner motivation to aim for success may diminish once those goals have been reached. For many people, motivation changes on arriving at a goal. Even though they have the capability of meeting similar future goals, they may have lost the drive to achieve them.

This issue is common in pop bands. Initially, they are driven by inner passion for success. Once they taste success, their world view can change. Even though the

30 R Meredith Belbin, Team Roles at Work, 2nd edition (Oxford: Butterworth-Heinemann Publications, 2010), p.22

The Art of Transformational Change

band has the capacity, it has lost the momentum to churn out more hits, and band members want a change in direction.

Successful football clubs in the English Premier League manage to dismantle their teams and still continue to achieve success. Table 10 compares the results of the premiership teams and the retention rates of players over four years. It is clear from this that there is no correlation between retention and success. Indeed Arsenal, which has retained players at almost seventy percent, has not won a title over that period.

Team	Percentage retained over 4 years from 09/10 to 12/13 season	Finishing position in Year12/13	Finishing position in year 11/12	Finishing position in year10/11
Manchester United	42.11%	1	2	1
Manchester City	26.32%	2	1	3
Chelsea	47.37%	3	6	2
Arsenal	68.42%	4	3	4
Tottenham Hotspur	36.84%	5	4	5
Everton	42.11%	6	7	7
Liverpool	47.37%	7	8	6
Fulham	36.84%	12	9	8
Aston Villa	21.05%	15	16	9
Sunderland	15.79%	17	13	10

Table 10: Retention of players versus finishing positions in the English Premiership

Should a winning team think about dismantling from the moment it is formed? This decision should be discussed openly from the outset, and written as part of the team formation. In many organisations, meeting forums and committees have no written definition of when they should dismantle. These committees often carry on past the point where they deliver positive benefits. Sometimes their continuation means that the benefit they initially created is lost; they become counterproductive.

Teams that are being dismantled must be given ample chance to "mourn", to capture learning and to bring awareness of differences in opinion or strategy which may have been revealed in the drive for success. This gives all members the chance to move on and start their next team with full focus and no lingering concerns.

Mourning can take place by being clear about dismantling at the outset (e.g. "Once we hit a particular success/goal/date, we will undertake the process of dismantling within an agreed timeframe."). This way it will not come as a surprise. I have seen many teams' members being forced to separate when the realisation came that the team had served its purpose or another project had been instigated. Another way is to celebrate and fix a date for the team to separate, even if there are small tasks left for individuals to complete: this definite date of completion provides certainty and closure.

Learning (see Chapter 3 on "Continuous Review") is an important aspect of capturing lessons. Creating a database of lessons learnt from every project team is important. It provides a mine of information for new teams.

The lessons might include things that were not voiced

between team members at the time. At the point of success, it is a good idea for the project manager to arrange for these unstated thoughts to be shared via feedback, on a one-to-one basis if necessary. It also means that awareness of subtle issues are raised, so that they don't subsequently become bigger problems.

How to create disparate HPTs

Face-to-face meetings remain important when dealing with critical decisions. Unstated thoughts and body language often provide crucial clues. However, if the team is located across multiple sites, technologies such as Skype, collaboration software and audio, make it possible to have four methods of team communication:

a Face-to-face – critical decisions and workshops for strategic planning, where group energy is required and used (possibly unconsciously) to make decisions.

b Video – team decisions which deal with diverse approaches or solutions.

c Audio – team updates/sharing information.

d Collaboration tools – information sharing and point communication.

In summary, there is a huge benefit to any kind of teamwork in an organisation, but in organisations that are adapting to a new world or going through intense change, a HPT creates the capability to absorb and implement change for sustainable outcomes. Having HPT's is likely to reduce the "waste" in implementation effort.

CHAPTER 6
TRIZ in Transformation

TRIZ, a Russian innovation and product-design process, has been recognised as a practical tool for use in Western society over the last ten years. It is a detailed method of delivering innovation to create new products. However, TRIZ can also be used effectively in transformative change, both in service design and change management.

It always astounds me when, on a warm summer's day, I see people choosing to run on a machine in a gym rather than enjoying a run in the park, a free and readily available resource! This choice is often based on the mindset that new innovations must be better as they are more complex than past methods, and of course this is not always the case. TRIZ is a tool that clarifies the contradictions which block innovations that could potentially employ free and readily available resources.

When organisations are faced with complex problems, they often call on experts or ask teams to brainstorm solutions; this can sometimes lead to an expensive mistake when ideas are adopted based on "copying" inventions that already exist. TRIZ helps remove the constraints that hinder innovation and get to entirely new solutions. It does not depend on a "eureka moment" or copying existing solutions to solve the problem. It seeks to work with the problem as part of the system it operates in.

TRIZ makes it easy to identify where a conflict or contradiction exists in the problem. Once the contradiction is understood, the method investigates whether both sides of the conflict can be satisfied without resorting to compromise. Where possible, this solution is attempted using freely available resources. When one considers available resources in an organisation, one often thinks of staff or budgets. However, in TRIZ, resources are much more widely considered; in particular, resources that are free and easily available are the first to be considered.

The best example of TRIZ in use in product design is from the book, *Simplified TRIZ* [31], in which there is an analysis of the design of an axe needed for intensive wood-chopping. Studying the purpose of the tool, it becomes clear that a contradiction exists, in that the axe should ideally be light but strong and highly durable. Thus, the contradiction statement "heavy axe versus light axe" symbolises the problems very well.

---

31 Source: Simplified TRIZ, Rantanen & Domb, Simplified TRIZ, (USA, Buca Raton: Auerbach Publications, 2008)

Figure 21: Finding the perfect axe

In this example, when all the freely available resources (energy, air, water) that might somehow solve the contradiction were considered, the idea of making the handle hollow, and filling it with air was eventually reached. This meant the axe head could still be mounted on a large handle, but the axe would be lighter and still as durable. This type of axe is now commonly available in the market. The example highlights how an innovative step solved a contradiction without compromise, and without the addition of a new component.

Twitter is another good example of a service innovation which could have been invented by TRIZ. As the internet developed and the "wow" factor passed in terms of volume of information, it became clear that many people could not cope with the vast amount of information arriving on their smart phones. Although the material was interesting, it was impossible to read everything. The same people still wanted to be connected with diverse ideas and opinions, leading to the contradiction: "lots of information versus little information". Twitter was the solution, providing highly-connected information between interested parties (lots of information) while being restricted to one hundred and forty characters (little information). Furthermore, the resource (the internet) is readily suited to sending text information to a number of devices without the need for highly-engineered software. Informa, a knowledge provider, predicts that forty-one billion messages will be sent over the internet, compared to almost twenty billion sent by direct mobile-to-mobile text messages every day.[32]

Case study – AMPLAMP

Figure 22: AMPLAMP Product

The amplamp was conceived in 2005 as a kind of bet during a series of TRIZ workshops run by Paul

---

32 Source: Informa, Press Release, 30 April 2013, http://informa.com/media/press-releases--news/latest-news/ott-messaging-traffic-will-be-twice-volume-of-p2p-sms-traffic-this-year/ [accessed 4 July 2014].

Frobisher, where an attendee suggested that Paul should take on a problem where there was limited background knowledge. Paul had just come across a new technology he was fascinated by – a type of speaker that used a totally different approach to producing sound. A traditional speaker uses a cone-shaped "driver" made out of light rigid material, to pump air in and out to create sound pressure waves. However new concepts had showed that a light, stiff panel can be made to vibrate chaotically, and Paul wondered what would happen if you apply the TRIZ tools to this technology, and evolve it in new directions. Paul worked on the idea of how a lamp which has redundant space within it, could be filled with the new type of speaker. So an under-utilised resource could be used for sound without the need for additional space or cables.

Retailers and specifiers all said they thought it was a "goer" as long as the aesthetics were uncompromised and audio was good enough to compare to the likes of Bose. At the *100% Design* show premier, the lighting buyer from Harrods saw the amplamp from a distance and was immediately interested in stocking it.

This is what TRIZ is all about – not accepting trade-off or compromise. The project achieved its product development goal, although sales were weak mainly due to the recession of 2008; culture and economic background plays a major part on good ideas becoming adapted.

So how do we apply the TRIZ tool in transformation processes? Some common conflicts that unfold are shown in Table 11.

Conflict statement	Contemplation of conflict
Financially proven benefit vs Substantial yet intangible benefit	Conflict in doing something that seems innately right versus time spent in creating a business case/cost-saving reasoning which is hard to grasp and measure.
Powerful leader vs Powerful teams	An all-powerful, charismatic leader versus teams that create future leaders and where leadership intuitively changes based on circumstances.
Energy in needs analysis vs Energy in solution design	Should we spend most of our time trying to understand and articulate needs thoroughly, in which case design and implementation become more straightforward, or should we build something 'on spec' then articulate the need?
Customers can never articulate what they want vs Customers must articulate what they want	Think about the solutions customers want rather than the design: a solution leads to a feature, which then leads to design. Customers can articulate which solutions will help them with their life/decisions; the company thinks about features and product design in light of this.
Resource spent managing stakeholders vs Resource in delivering a product	Sometimes delivering a product gives you an easier way to engage with stakeholders.
Error-free solution vs Error-tolerant solution	Where there are high interactions in system dynamics, errors are bound to occur (for example it is impossible to predict the weather accurately). In this case, build error-tolerant solutions; remove repetitive and predictable errors.

Conflict statement	Contemplation of conflict
Processes need to be standard vs Processes need to be flexible	Some things need to be done at the same standard for health and safety reasons; in this case you don't want deviation. Imposing a standard where human beings are involved is not necessary, as long as the outcome is consistent and repeatable. Think about the outcome as much as the process and open yourself to different ways of working.
Fast decision-making vs Deliberative decision-making	This conflict often occurs in organisations that need to act quickly and decisively to make sure faith and trust in management is not lost. Yet there is also a need to be deliberative and consider the full systematic implications of their decision-making

Table 11: Examples of conflict in change programmes

In many transformations, getting to "good enough" can take a long time due to the fact that errors are inherent. Overall system dynamics are always changing; it is impossible to achieve perfection. Some errors don't surface until implementation if the solution is complex. Error-tolerant solutions, on the other hand, assume that errors are likely to occur and prepare for the worst. This can lead to a lack of emphasis on perfecting the design or a lack of proper testing, as people work on the assumption that problems will be "sorted on the day". Thus, the contradictory statement "error-free solution versus error-tolerant solution" becomes the starting point for innovation.

How to resolve conflicts

Step one is to change the contradictory "or" statement to an "and" statement. For example, the question included in the example above should be: "How can we have both error-free *and* error-tolerant solutions?" Sometimes, by just adding *and*, an intuitive leap to the answer can be created.

In transformation, the resources that are "invisible", inexpensive or freely available are often not considered. These include resources such as customers, stakeholders, internal experts, the layout of office space, and "open" or free-to-use software that has been developed by collaborative voluntary effort. Industry has come a long way in stakeholder-management: customers themselves now provide useful (and mostly free) insight. Most transformation programmes have highly active stakeholder-management teams working in continuous partnership.

The weaknesses in resource management tend to centre on the ways an organisation manages its own employees, many of whom have diverse skills, some latent which are never given a chance to shine. Often, once people have entered a large organisation in a specific role, they are "labelled" with a narrow set of skills. Their full range of traits and latent skills are never given rein. HR departments can act as a barrier as they hold only details of demonstrated skills. This in turn, rather than aiding the process of discovering the right person, can strangle the process of finding the right skills to meet the current situation. When a need for these resources arises, knowledge of who is available can be lacking. The system might not encourage experts to "volunteer" for projects or pieces of work. So a starting point is for HR to consider what "freely available" staff resources exist. In doing so, they may find solutions to problems that require different support: providing both recruitment and skills advice to departments, for example, rather than just recruitment. In this way HR departments can become powerful and pro-active in supporting businesses rather than sometimes being perceived as a bureaucracy, a route to recruitment or helping with point solutions only.

TRIZ recognises that many resources are in plentiful supply; it is just a matter of tapping into them with new insight. For example, an organisation could create a culture where people can volunteer to join fixed-period projects rather than waiting to be chosen. In fixed-period projects, commitment can be managed. Collaborative tools that engage the workforce can be used. 3M, an organisation that designs innovative product materials and technology, is a good example where employees are allowed fifteen percent free time to explore projects of their own choosing. Google also has something similar called "twenty-percent time" to spend time on projects that are outside of their standard job descriptions.

In short, before tapping into expensive paid resources, an organization should explore how it can first utilise resources which are freely available. This will enable organisations to first "look in" rather than "look out" for resources.

Conflict in decision-making, that never gets addressed, can result in projects that achieve poor benefit. The NHS

Programme "Connecting for Health" is a good example, where fast decision-making proved to be disastrous.[33] The project spent more than half of the £12 billion programme budget with, overall, over seventy percent of the work still outstanding in 2011; in many cases not even a single care record system was delivered. The main reasons for failing to deliver benefit were: trying to impose systems on practitioners which they had not bought in to, dealing with suppliers in adversarial ways, and thinking that such a big programme could be implemented without prototyping or testing on a smaller scale.

In preparation for the 2011 census in England and Wales, the government census board grappled with ways in which to deal with the intensive operational period when questionnaires were being sent out, returned and processed. They wanted to increase the speed of decision-making, yet ensure that they made deliberated and careful decisions. How could they insure against avoidable risks, yet take appropriate risks during a fast-moving operation?

Using the AND analogy, they set up structures that allowed both aspects to be met. "Take risks, avoid risks" is a good contradiction statement. The structure they created allowed decision-making by senior executives. This was followed by a meeting with the board to seek assurance around those decisions. This meant that decision-making was fast and effective. It had a proper

---

33 'The National Programme for IT in the NHS: an update on the delivery of detailed care records systems', National Audit Office, 18 May 2011, http://www.nao.org.uk/report/the-national-programme-for-it-in-the-nhs-an-update-on-the-delivery-of-detailed-care-records-systems/ [accessed 5 June 2014].

consideration of resources (high-quality people with the in-depth knowledge and ability to understand systematic issues) to run a series of cascaded meetings. The result was "on-the-day" decisions followed by an assurance board that probed but did not overturn decisions unless absolutely necessary.

Figure 23: TRIZ allows conflict to be resolved

Another element of TRIZ is to consider resource at two levels. Free resources can emerge from higher-level systems (e.g. customer processes, the product use etc.). Alternatively, such resources can come from a subsystem, one of the components of the system itself. The wind-up radio makes use of a source of free energy (from stored energy in a human) to wind up a spring to provide battery power to a radio. As an example for transformation, consider whether the geometry of a room (the subsystem) can provide a different resource (e.g. an innovation room). The Apple iPhone is a good example of a product that uses a free resource at the micro-level: the casing itself is the aerial.

In process-improvement work, many organisations become so busy addressing customer complaints that they have no time to appreciate their existing needs and invent new products or services to cater to them. This results in the contradiction statement "less customer contact versus more customer contact". One way to create new products can be to involve the customer in defining and voting on features for new products, involving them fully in the design. In this case, the customer is the readily available resource. In contrast, other companies create intensive customer handling systems, focus groups or expensive market research to seek the same results, which can be expensive and sometimes self-serving. Organisations often seek complex IT tools for advanced project-planning systems and use a standard, very linear, process that flows as shown below:

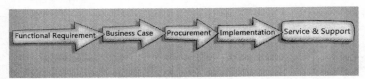

Figure 24: Traditional process for choosing IT/Technology

Organisations are not set up to procure freely available or 'agile' based software and mechanisms cannot procure something that is not "fully defined". Such a process could exist and I believe it would look like the one in Figure 25.

Figure 25: A better way of choosing IT technology

The biggest benefit is that the procurement and design

processes are intertwined and can be stopped at any part of the chain. Benefits include building a design that is fit for purpose as well as for working in full collaboration with suppliers. Extensive and relatively cheap web based software tools now exist to help with collaboration.

During transformational change projects, the contradiction of making meetings flow and keeping them short, while still making good decisions, can be solved by having standing meetings. This helps create energy and momentum.

Solving problems at a higher-system level

One method of using TRIZ is to identify whether a problem must be solved at a subsystem level or at a higher system level. For example, a major car rental company in the UK had an issue with the turnaround of cars during peak hours. Each car needed cleaning and washing, with additional time allowed for it to be driven to and from the wash centre.

At this system level, solutions such as *Lean*[34] could help with quickening the cleaning cycle and improving the drumbeat of available cars. But at the higher-system level of analysing customer needs, the company realised that cars returned in the same day, particularly during winter, did not need the same level of cleaning and washing. Most business customers accepted a car with a thoroughly clean interior but unwashed exterior,

---

34 James Womack and Daniel Jones, Lean Thinking: Banish Waste and Create Wealth in Your Corporation, (London: Simon and Schuster, 2003).

as long as there was no obvious dirt, because they used their cars during low daylight hours. By focusing on the higher system (the customer), the whole system of external cleaning was eliminated for cars that were in "good enough" condition, resulting in reducing costs and improved turnaround time.

TRIZ has many aspects, but the most important thing to identify during transformative change is the contradiction. What ideal result do you want and what resources are cheaply or freely available to help resolve the contradiction? With TRIZ, you are not trying to compromise; you are trying to find the "and" to resolve the conflict at another level.

In summary, TRIZ offers three different sets of thinking for transformation change:

- It forces one to identify conflicts that exist in a transformation project, set out a contradiction statement and consider how both ends of the conflict can be met without compromise.

- It starts with the assumption that freely available resources can be used to resolve the conflict.

- It investigates whether the problem can be solved at a higher system level, or at a micro-system level, in which the components of the system are a part of the solution.

CHAPTER 7
Systems Thinking

Many of the work-streams of delivery are assumed to be directly related within large-scale transformations (one output forms the input to another) rather than systematically related (inputs and outputs are linked and multidirectional). Support functions, along with the organisation's underlying culture and ways of working, have a deeper effect on the overall system than might be assumed at first glance. Systems thinking is very different from a dependency diagram that sticks to tasks and activities.

Systems thinking examines the factors in play during a transformation and tries to discover the connections between them. In practice, the work stream elements of transformation, organisation support functions and culture and behaviour that drive outcomes overlap.

Key characteristics of systems

In systems, many elements interact in many ways. The attributes of the elements and interactions between them are imprecise or ambiguous. There is a variance in behaviour, with the result that the same outcome is unlikely even when the input is the same. Take weather systems in the UK — it is difficult to predict the exact outcome even if two fronts are exactly the same at two different points, i.e. they have the same start conditions. Systems are also subject to the way people within the system direct them or make decisions. So a teacher's behaviour and attitude has a big impact on the school system, over and above the teacher's competence, the school's facilities, governance, teaching aids, materials etc. Finally the system is impacted by external factors: it is not closed.

The lack of understanding of systems causes unexpected consequences, through a lack of knowledge of the underlying levers that trigger the outcomes. However they often become clear after the event.

In the UK, for chronic health delivery, there are many organisations involved (primary, secondary and tertiary care providers), many stakeholders (patients, their relatives, carers, GPs), and many variations (every patient is different). At the same time deprivation, overall health and many other factors come into play. The lack of a systems thinking approach creates processes that only work for a cohort and can create unexpected consequences.

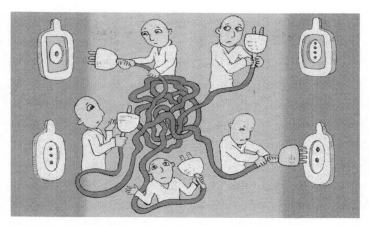

Figure 26: Processes can be complex systems

Many hospitals have no systems map of the way in which theatres, patient flow, A&E, medical wards and employee morale are connected.

There are many books about systems thinking in reference to complexity; but the question is, how can this be tied to transformative change?

A systems analysis shows how processes or drivers of processes are interlinked as well as the importance of systems thinking during the transformation process. The creation of a highly visual systems map helps organisations appreciate the "whole". It enables a capture of ambiguity and the understanding of vagueness of the effect of changes in one factor on another, and creates the crucial questions whose answers give a better understanding of connections.

Systems thinking map identifies root causes

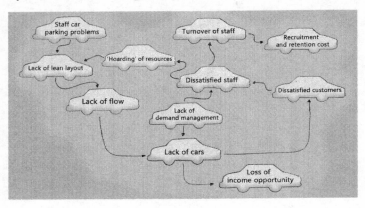

Figure 27: Systems diagram for car rental company

In a process-improvement example for a car rental business, the team looked at the key issues that the processes created. It then looked at underlying factors and how these factors might be interlinked. The factors were gathered by looking at the issues that cause problems and any factors associated with them. In this case, it became clear that lack of staff parking plus lack of demand management had created unintended consequences. Although the team would have liked to examine lack of flow (the classic thing to look at) it became clear that resolving staff parking issues, perhaps as part of the car compound layout, needed to be addressed first. After this a more linear process to improve car flow could be taken.

While the interdependence of factors can be vague, with no particular "equation" of consequences, further clarity can be gained by understanding whether the impact would be positive or negative. It also enables one to see the big picture of the activities and ensures the mind is looking at evidence and solutions to improve the whole process.

Creating a systems map in a large-scale transformation

An understanding of the drivers and factors for change in the organisation is essential. The next step is to connect them. Although these factors may be relatively standard, the ways in which they connect is the crucial point. Let's take the scenario of a hospital that has difficulty in recruiting nurses where finances are poor but standards/governance is good. The first thing to think about is the impact of vacancies on the end goal of the organisation and how they are linked to other factors.

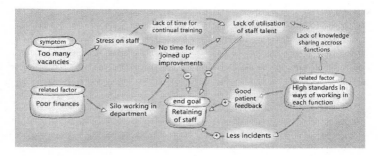

Figure 28: Systems map for retaining staff in an NHS Trust

Once you have a map, albeit fuzzy, a discussion of cause and effect can take place. System maps can show where there is a turning point that could lead to significant benefit or catastrophic disaster. In the case in Figure 28, staff involvement is the key factor that affects the system.

Systems thinking allows decisions to be made with the benefit of a systems map, so that unintended consequences can be reflected in the overall system. This ensures resources are not focused on an activity with short-term benefit, but look at the 'bigger picture'.

Figure 29: Making the connections in a system

Once these connections are discovered they can be employed for consultation with stakeholders so that cause and effect is better understood and managed: for example, accurate weather forecasting is very difficult, and better managed by informing people of the probability of weather conditions so that they can manage their own situation by carrying umbrellas, or buying sun cream etc.

The costs of unintended consequences can be huge. The systematic failure of the banking sector to manage its assets and liabilities cost the taxpayer £124bn[35] in borrowed cash and the banking sector £9bn in fees.

35 Central Finance and Treasury, "Maintaining the financial stability of UK banks: update on support schemes". www.nao.org.uk. June 2014

At the Mid Staffordshire NHS Trust, a hospital that systematically failed in 2008, 400–1200 more patients died between 2005–2008 than expected.[36]

"It is clear... the system as a whole failed in its most essential duty... to protect patients from unacceptable risks of harm and from unacceptable, and in some cases inhumane, treatment".

−Francis Report [37]

Enquiries and reconfiguration of systematic failure, are likely to cost the taxpayer tens of millions of pounds. The impact on the communities and families who use the hospital is likely to be high but hard to measure accurately.

Various modelling tools can be used if system dynamics become unclear. The best option, where possible, is to have pilots or tests on the systems to study the effects. Systems maps also need to consider seemingly unconnected forces to see if there is a hidden connection that can be empirically tested.

A test can identify "pinch points" or critical relationships that affect the overall system. This should move the focus for improvement to where it is needed rather than where the symptom of failure occurs.

A difference in opinion between the people who map the flows or the strength of the connections provides an ideal opportunity to investigate and improve the systems map. In fact, systems maps are never right first time, they need the rigour of analysis and contemplation.

36 Report of Mid Staffordshire NHS Foundation Trust Public Enquiry, chaired by Robert Francis, (London: The Stationary Office, 2013).

37 Report of Mid Staffordshire NHS Foundation Trust Public Enquiry, chaired by Robert Francis, (London: The Stationary Office, 2013).

The systems map should be "live". It is dynamic and should be able to change rapidly or slowly, based on what is happening "on the ground".

Improvement can be directed to the areas which contribute maximum systematic benefit. There needs to be proper attribution and a better opportunity to review accurately. People often make assumptions in hindsight about the factor that made things improve, and a systems map is a good way to demonstrate whether the improvement was due to the attributed factors or not.

In systems thinking, we study whole systems, particularly where properties cannot be identified, by the examination of the separate actions of the parts. Systemic properties are derived from the interaction of the parts in the system, not from the separate actions of those parts. For any activity, seek to understand in what containing system the activity you are interested in sits, and understand the behaviour or properties of the containing system. If possible eliminate the effect of problems in a system by designing it in a way that has the problem already built into it. For example, imbalance is already built into a bicycle, which ensures that riders have to continuously balance themselves. This is similar to preventing a disease by inoculation. It is more efficient than curing a problem once it has occurred.

In summary, systems thinking is about becoming aware of the pinch points in the system, and seeking to modify or having proper risk management plans for them, or indeed leveraging any benefits. It helps better understand which small deviations can create a large output change.

CHAPTER 8
Fast Failure and Fast Learning

Organisations are facing complexities like never before. Complications have increased over the last thirty years in internal processes fuelled by complexity of technology, and product variation. Customers have become more fickle: they have high expectations which are constantly changing. There are more players and components in the system: IT systems, suppliers, legislation and governance. The interaction creates complexity and sometimes conflict. In addition the costs of failure are high to both the organisation and the customer as dependency on complex products grows. Sub-systems themselves have become more complex: for example, documentation is no longer on paper, but on IT servers.

For example, people have become extremely reliant on mobile phones, which are now deemed to be essential; if mobile services are not available, dissatisfaction is immense. The failure of Blackberry systems in 2011 for a period of two days shows the amount of dissatisfaction that can be caused by a short failure of what people consider essential. The failure of a subsystem can now affect the whole system.

As discussed in Chapter 7, these complexities create effects on the overall system which cannot be resolved solely at a logical level. They also have outcomes that cannot be guaranteed. However, they can be understood by analysing the system. An organisation focused on functional excellence is not enough; there must be an awareness of the whole system. Ensuring end-to-end excellence becomes crucial.

These issues have also emerged in the public sector and government departments. There is now a huge expectation for delivering services with value for money as well as speed of delivery. In the UK, there has also been large, IT-enabled change that has consumed enormous resources as the complexity of the projects have become clear. The NHS "Connecting for Health" project, which had as its core vision every patient having an electronic care record that could be shared between all service providers, started with a full project cost of £5bn[38] over three years, which rose to a projected cost of £11.4bn[39] over ten years by the National Audit Office, with the government's own select committee stating that:

---

38 Ted Ritter, "Proof that NPFIT programme was supposed to be £5B". Computer Weekly, 6 April 2009, http://www.computerweekly.com/blogs/public-sector/2009/04/proof-that-npfit-cost-was-put.html [accessed 5 June 2014].

39 "The National Programme for IT in the NHS: an update on the delivery of detailed care records systems". National Audit Office, 18 May 2011, http://www.nao.org.uk/report/the-national-programme-for-it-in-the-nhs-an-update-on-the-delivery-of-detailed-care-records-systems/# [accessed 5 June 2014]

'Four years after the start of the Programme, there is still much uncertainty about the costs of the Programme for the local NHS and the value of the benefits it should achieve'.[40]

Organisations need to consider a different method of testing customer requirements when managing transformational change or complex programme delivery. In transformational change and in new-process design, testing is often limited to one level (e.g. software, specific processes or a proof of concept), or done in a way that tests a single tool, solution or IT aspect. This approach lacks an overview of seeing where the bigger system might fail. Tests of a wide range of scenarios, reflecting real life, are where the best lessons are to be learnt. The greatest learning is a result of stress testing.

Business process testing is often considered at the end of the design, rather than as part of it. In fact, end-to-end process testing is best carried out throughout the design. There is an implied contradiction here – how can you test a design without it being complete?

The use of piloting to understand a new process or structure by instinct is as important a skill as thinking. This instinct or intuition can be used to become aware of all of the interconnections between system components and possible outcomes. Some leaders are naturally gifted at doing this and following through

40 House of Commons Committee of Public Accounts, Department of Health: The National Programme of IT in the NHS,(London: The Stationary Office Limited, 2007), http://www.publications.parliament.uk/pa/cm200607/cmselect/cmpubacc/390/390.pdf [accessed 5 June 2014]

by using logic to demonstrate this intuition. However, many organisations disapprove of illogical or "fuzzy" thought, meaning that the trait is often not encouraged. As an example, the intuition that "something worried me about this, but I don't know what" is not recognised as valuable.

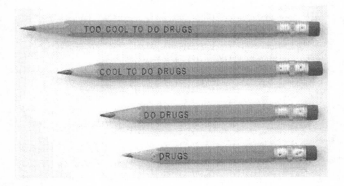

Figure 30: The pencil with the wrong message. Source Brrybnds

Figure 30 is a perfect example of the lack of testing to discover fast failure. These pencils were sent to a New York school in the late nineties and had to be returned, with plenty of embarrassment, because as the pencil got sharpened the message got subverted, as can be seen above.[41] A simple "fast failure" test considering the end-to-end processes would have revealed the problem quickly.

One way of piloting is to test different levels of design, for example, by a walkthrough. This may show which parts of the design are not complete, expose new

41 'Slogan causes pencil recall', New York Times, December 1998, http://www.nytimes.com/1998/12/12/nyregion/slogan-causes-pencil-recall.html [accessed 5 June 2014]

issues, or even suggest certain elements of the design that are not required or add little value.

Study on the opening of Terminal 5

British Airways and BAA, the airport operating authority, opened Terminal 5 at Heathrow Airport in March 2008 with great fanfare. Fourteen thousand bags were stranded and four hundred flights cancelled with the cost to BA estimated between £16m and £50m plus reputational damage.[42] Deutsche Bank forecast that the problems at Terminal 5 would cost the airline about £150m in total.[43]

> *Throughout early morning and afternoon, two overarching factors contributed to the delays. According to industry sources, some baggage teams were disorientated despite months of training and were late turning up at loading areas, which are spaced around the cavernous baggage area. Plus, there was a shortage of special storage bins that all bags must be put in before going onto planes – a new requirement for T5.*[44]

42 Dan Milmo, "T5 Fiasco costs BA £16m", The Guardian, 03 April 2008, http://www.theguardian.com/business/2008/apr/03/britishairwaysbusiness.theairlineindustry [accessed 2 June 2015]

43 "BA Terminal 5 losses top £16m", BBC, 03 April 2008, http://news.bbc.co.uk/2/hi/business/7328838.stm [accessed 5 June 2014]

44 Dan Milmo, "Catalogue of errors' led to T5 fiasco", The Guardian, 28 March 2008, http://www.theguardian.com/business/2008/mar/28/theairlineindustry.britishairwaysbusiness2 [accessed 5 June 2014]

British Airways did not spot systematic issues before the T5 disaster. In fact, they did not practise a full rollout – the work they had done a few weeks previously was not a proper end-to-end test.

Employees arriving for work could not find their way to the staff car park. Road signs outside the terminal were not clear, and people said they were given wrong directions once inside.

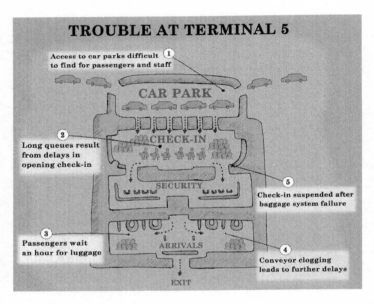

Figure 31: Terminal 5 – Issues on the first day of opening

Once a system has been studied and specific but unpredictable issues that may arise identified, one option is to "inoculate" the problem as part of the system, a "vaccination" as it were. In the case of British Airways and BAA, they had set up a series of public trials. The trials may have succeeded in identifying improvements and enabling members of the public to experience the new terminal, but they failed in the ultimate objective of testing 'end-to-end' processes to a point where it worked well enough to cope with the opening successfully. The issue of staff being unable to arrive on time the first day due to traffic congestion may have not been foreseen, but the system could have been inoculated by free transport or even a free taxi service.

Willie Walsh, CEO of BA stated: "My regret is that we did compromise on the testing programme [...] we knew this was a risk; it was a calculated risk and a risk that I agreed to take".[45]

BA and BAA admit that they did not carry out a stress test of "real-life" scenarios, particularly around baggage handling, and did not consider the other factors in place. Colin Matthews, CEO of BAA, said: "It may have been that the baggage we were testing was too uniform [...] maybe the reality of the baggage that people put into the system was more diverse than our tests represented".

---

45 House of Commons Transport Committee, The Opening of Heathrow Terminal T5, (London: Stationery Office, 2008: Page 5).

Figure 32: Lack of end-to-end testing for Terminal 5 opening

The problem of staff car parking could have been solved by giving staff a free travel ticket for the transportation system of their choice, so the problem of car parking would never have arisen in the first place. People always feel disorientated in a new place (despite any signage on the walls); a team whose sole responsibility is to guide people to the "obvious" becomes necessary. In this case, extra and very visible signage for *staff car park* or *passenger car park*, people standing on the roads to help, and even a one-off guided marked line to the car park ("Follow the blue line") could have solved the problem.

For the successful England and Wales national census of 2011, the Office for National Statistics set up various scenarios and exercises to ensure that during its peak of field operational work, they could sense what unfolding events might mean in terms of decision-making and thinking.

Setting up end-to-end process tests

While there are many ways to do this, one classic way is to walk through all the processes with an end-to-end point of view. An alternative is to build a complex "day in the life" of an individual as they use the system to see what obstacles confront them. A third way is to do a "what if" analysis, considering all variations of inputs to see if the system can adapt. One can also set up a scenario with actors in a classroom exercise to test the decision-making of key players. The Emergency Planning Society creates tests such as these to assess the readiness of UK emergency services for major crises.

Before running an end-to-end process test ask these questions:

- How can the process be tested to get real insight?
- Which exercise would work well at this stage of the activities?
- What is the start and end point of your process test?
- How can you test the process to understand the point of failure?

Agree parameters and ensure that the assumptions of your test processes are set out and understood by the people who are front line (not the designers). Have a clear definition of what area of processes will be tested. Finally, write down your scenario for the process and the start point of the test. Include moments of humour in the script, as well as real world events (e.g. someone being ill) to make the scenarios realistic.

During testing, brief the participants in advance. Where possible identify what roles they want to undertake. Ensure that you have set out clear ground rules and expectations, so that everyone is participating with the same understanding. These scenarios, although not real, can still be very uncomfortable, even if the lesson in hindsight seems obvious. In my experience people at all levels of an organisation will get some benefit (though they might not admit to it) by being part of such a scenario.

Some people like to plant "red herrings" in scenarios – these can be useful but don't overdo them. Where possible, go beyond a simple communication setting, such as a meeting; include telephone calls, emails etc. to make the test realistic. Ensure that there is a logbook in which to record activities as they occur. Spend at least thirty percent of the time on feedback and lessons learnt by reviewing the activities.

After the testing, update risk registers and share the lessons learnt widely. Agree the priorities required for change in processes, specifications and standards, and decide what test(s) you need to run again and when.

Another way of testing is to ask rigorous questions of the design team to force them to consider the "end-to-end" process. A good question is: "How could I make this design fail in practice?"

It is important to identify the key influencers and protagonists, and get them involved in the test of the design or idea. If possible, pinpoint the people who are always full of criticism in the organisation and ask them to find weaknesses in the design (with the caveat that you can ignore their criticism if need be). People are often so attached to their own ideas that they do not seek out criticism.

Involve the customer early on, taking care to make it clear that you are at an early phase of work. An emphatic customer will love to be part of the design process and can provide objective insight.

Understand (see Chapter 1 on "Dimensional Value") which areas of failure of value/features impact customers the most and their relative importance.

A failure means that the assumptions made in design or execution were wrong. Fixing problems and learning from failure may still lead to unexpected outcomes. The components of the systems may interact in a different way. Furthermore, the external start point may be different (e.g. a simple matter such as weather conditions might create a different external outcome). Hence, assumptions need to be validated and consideration needs to be given to complex systems (see Chapter 7 on Systems Thinking).

In summary, fast failure and fast learning is all about learning by 'end-to-end' testing. By experimentation using real processes/systems at an early stage one is able to get a true idea of a process that is impacted by business transformation. Too often the use of only abstract review of transformational design inhibits this learning.

CONCLUSION

Throughout this book, I have tried to show techniques that can be used at any point during a large-scale transformation programme to provide deep insight, yet are not overtly difficult to use. All of them take on complex areas of a business and have the ability to show not just the connections and areas that need addressing, but a potential way of moving forward.

All transformation programmes need three elements to succeed: planning for transformation; processes and methods to achieve change; and a plan for sustainability. This book provides techniques that are useful across all three areas. The techniques are standalone but can also be used in conjunction with others.

Which technique to use?

Here is a summary that will help decide which techniques you can use when faced with specific problems or situations. It shows the approach or context of using each technique, how and when to use it and how it might work in combination with another technique(s). Table 12 shows which techniques you can use when faced with specific problems or situations.

Chapter 1 – Using Dimensional Values

How and when to use this technique:

- Use Dimensional Values in a focus group or a questionnaire approach, to understand different aspects of value that customers and/or producers have around products or services.

Context in transformation:

- Use at the onset of transformational change to ensure value perceptions of change to the end customer are documented and discussed.

Combination with other techniques:

- Consider during Continuous Review to ensure that the business processes are delivering value.
- Resolution of conflicts in meeting Dimensional Values for customers can be done using TRIZ.

Chapter 2 – Systematic Clearing Out

How and when to use this technique:

- Systematic Clearing Out of materials and information is important because it allows a focus on critical memory and removes unimportant data that causes an undercurrent of frustration and tension.
- Hands on – everyone in the function is involved.

Context in transformation:

- Helps decide which knowledge and material

must go and which to retain or embed during a transformational programme.

- Helps reduce organisation stress and improve motivation.

Combination with other techniques:

- Works well as a specific activity within Continuous Review.

Chapter 3 – Continuous Review

How and when to use this technique:

- Continuous Review is a building block that makes an organisation more aware at all levels about its current state and helps identify problems early.
- An excellent way of making teams stop to take stock; stops mindless impetus to transformational change.

Context in transformation:

- Helps identify "how things are" in their fullest before undertaking action.
- Allows the possibility of bringing about awareness with no action – stops needless activity.

Combination with other techniques:

- Systems Thinking maps can be used as part of a Continuous Review of processes.
- A regular activity of High Performing Teams is Continuous Review.

- Systematic Clearing Out can be a specific activity as part of Continuous Review.

Chapter 4 – RACI

How and when to use this technique:

- RACI (Responsibility, Accountability, Consultation and Information) is a management tool which is extremely useful as an enabler in deciding "who does what" at different hierarchies of activities.
- A living tool – RACIs change with time and needs frequent revising.

Context in transformation:

- In complex transformational change there are many "players" and clarity is needed about who is doing the work and who is giving advisory information.
- Allows subsidiarity – better decision-making from bottom up.

Combination with other techniques:

- Can work well with Continuous Review in having clarity in who does what.
- Works well with Creating High Performance Teams.

Chapter 5 – Creating and Dismantling High Performance Teams

How and when to use this technique:

- High performing "on-the-ground" teams are essential ingredients for managing the constant change that businesses face today.

- Used by leaders and managers in creating the right team structure.

Context in transformation

- Brings clarity around structure for transformational teams to succeed.

- Enables dismantling of teams and a full review of past success and failure.

Combination with other techniques:

- Using RACI can help ensure teams have got the right roles and are working to their optimum.

Chapter 6 – TRIZ in Transformation

How and when to use this technique:

- TRIZ is a tool that clarifies the contradictions of a problem and leads to innovation.

- Use in a workshop style with strong facilitation.

Context in transformation:

- When there is conflict between transformation work streams and problems seem impossible to solve.

- When costs of solutions are very expensive and cheaper ideas are needed.

Combination with other techniques:

- Works well when using Understanding Dimensional Values to help drive better solutions in new design.

Chapter 7 – Systems Thinking

How and when to use this technique:

- Systems Thinking examines the factors at play during a transformation and tries to discover the connections between them.
- Create highly visual flows mapped on a large whiteboard or 'brown paper' wall.

Context in transformation:

- Allows the understanding of joins in complex transformation – what impacts what, even if the level of impact is ambiguous.
- Allows better decision-making about where to apply change.
- Clarifies risk and purpose early.

Combination with other techniques:

- Works well in conjunction with Fast Failure and Fast Learning, and Continuous Review.

Chapter 8 – Fast Failure and Fast Learning

How and when to use this technique:

- Fast Failure and Fast Learning works well when testing end-to-end processes/systems to get a true idea of how processes are impacted by business transformation.

- Use to prove the flow of process at various stages of design.

Context in transformation:

- Quickly identifies gaps in flows of new processes or products, as part of transformation, to see the 'whole'.

- Changes mindset when looking at a significant operational change.

- Highly flexible and leveraged – testing becomes bigger and better prior to 'going live'.

Combination with other techniques:

- Can be used by understanding failure or opportunities as part of Systems Thinking.

Technique/ Transformational challenge	Clarity in scope and benefit	Leadership & Ownership	Stakeholder engagement	Managing disparate resources	Risk/Contingency management	Innovation	Applying best practice
1 Using Dimensional Values	X		X		X	X	
2 Systematic Clearing Out	X		X				X
3 Continuous Review	X	X	X		X		X
4 RACI		X	X	X	X		
5 Creating & Dismantling High Performing Teams		X		X	X	X	X
6 TRIZ in Transformation			X			X	
7 Systems Thinking	X		X	X	X	X	X
8 Fast Failure and Fast Learning	X		X	X	X	X	X

Table 12: Interventions for different transformational challenges

ABOUT THE AUTHOR

Ketan Varia is the founder of Kinetik Solutions and has over 25 years of Management and Consulting experience. He is focused on leading and guiding strategy and improvement programmes within an operational context.

He has led over 30 change assignments, across ten countries, for a variety of FT Global 500 companies at Kinetik and in previous roles at Capgemini and Ernst & Young.

His extensive experience includes development projects with ADP, Abbey National, British Airways, BAE, Blind Veterans UK, EMI Music, Hertz, Office for National Statistics, Land Rover, Motorola, several NHS Trusts, Nations Trust Bank, Network Rail and Xerox.

Ketan is a former non-executive director for The North West London Hospitals Trust, where he sat on their Audit and Governance & Risk Committees. He is also a Chartered Engineer, a Fellow of the Royal Society of Arts and a Fellow of the Institute of Operational Management.

He is an active volunteer in neighbourhood mediation, an engineering ambassador for STEMNET, and provides mentoring for members of the Prince's Trust and the Institute for Engineering and Technology (IET).

INDEX

A

B

C

D

E

F
Failure 14, 16, 47, 56, 108, 109, 111, 114, 119, 121, 126, 128
Features (of product or service) 21-29, 31, 32, 100

G
Governance 55, 69, 104, 107, 111

I
Idea(s) 36, 78, 80, 81, 89, 91, 93, 121, 127
Impact (of change) 14, 16, 47, 54, 104, 106, 107, 109, 121, 127, 128
Implementation (of change) 12, 36, 46, 57, 80, 88, 95
Individual (affect on) 14, 28, 31, 36, 38, 39, 40, 43, 59, 60, 63, 67, 68, 70, 77, 78, 80, 84, 85, 119
Innovation 12, 38, 89-91, 95, 99, 126

L
Leadership 15, 46, 67, 80, 84, 94

M
Management (managers) 11, 14-17, 42, 43, 48-50, 56, 59, 62, 67, 72, 73, 75, 79, 88, 89, 96, 125, 126,129
Meeting(s) 43, 49, 53, 79, 84, 87, 88, 99, 101
Momentum 37, 43, 45, 46-48, 60, 86, 101
Motivation 17, 60, 73, 75, 80, 85, 124

O
Olympics 54, 55
Operational 50, 65, 78, 98, 118, 128, 131

P
Patients 23, 25, 31, 32, 33, 48, 51, 52, 104, 105, 109, 112
Performance (measurement of) 13, 16, 47
Piloting 113, 114
Problem-solving 16, 37, 49, 82, 101
Purpose 35, 40, 66, 73, 75, 84, 87, 90, 101, 127

Q
Quality 33, 60, 69, 73

49576302R00083

Made in the USA
Charleston, SC
28 November 2015